The Liberating Power of Symbols

Books by Jürgen Habermas included in the series
Studies in Contemporary German Social Thought
Thomas McCarthy, general editor

Jürgen Habermas, *Between Facts and Norms: Contributions to a Discourse Theory of Law and Democracy*
Jürgen Habermas, *Justification and Application: Remarks on Discourse Ethics*
Jürgen Habermas, *On the Logic of the Social Sciences*
Jürgen Habermas, *The Inclusion of the Other: Studies in Political Theory*
Jürgen Habermas, *The Liberating Power of Symbols: Philosophical Essays*
Jürgen Habermas, *Moral Consciousness and Communicative Action*
Jürgen Habermas, *The New Conservatism: Cultural Criticism and the Historians' Debate*
Jürgen Habermas, *The Philosophical Discourse of Modernity: Twelve Lectures*
Jürgen Habermas, *Philosophical-Political Profiles*
Jürgen Habermas, *Postmetaphysical Thinking: Philosophical Essays*
Jürgen Habermas, *The Postnational Constellation: Political Essays*
Jürgen Habermas, *On the Pragmatics of Communication*
Jürgen Habermas, *On the Pragmatics of Social Interaction: Preliminary Studies in the Theory of Communicative Action*
Jürgen Habermas, *The Structural Transformation of the Public Sphere: An Inquiry into a Category of Bourgeois Society*
Jürgen Habermas, editor, *Observations on "The Spiritual Situation of the Age"*

The Liberating Power of Symbols

Philosophical Essays

Jürgen Habermas

translated by Peter Dews

The MIT Press

Cambridge, Massachusetts

First MIT Press edition, 2001
Copyright © this translation Polity Press 2001. First published in
Germany as *Vom sinnlichen Eindruck zum symbolischen Ausdruck* ©
Suhrkamp Verlag 1997.

Library of Congress Cataloging-in-Publication Data

Habermas, Jürgen,
    [Vom sinnilichen Eindruck zum symbolischen Ausdruck English]
    The liberating power of symbols: philosophical essays /
Jürgen Habermas; translated by Peter Dews—1st MIT Press ed.
    p. cm.—(Studies in contemporary German social thought)
    Includes bibliographical references (p.) and index.
    Contents: The liberating power of symbols—The conflict of beliefs—
Between traditions—Tracing the other of history in history—A master
builder with hermeneutic tact—Israel or Athens, where does
anamnestic reason belong?—Communicative freedom and negative
theology—The useful mole who ruins the beautiful lawn.
    ISBN 0-262-08296-9 (hc.: alk. paper)—ISBN 0-262-58205-8
(pbk.: alk. paper)
    1. Philosophy. I. Title. II. Series.

B3258.H322 E5 2001
193–dc21

                                            00-048962

Typeset in 11 on 13 pt Berling
by Kolam Information Services Private Ltd, Pondicherry, India.
Printed in Great Britain by TJ International, Padstow, Cornwall

This book is printed on acid-free paper.

Contents

Preface   vi

1   The Liberating Power of Symbols   1
Ernst Cassirer's Humanistic Legacy and the
Warburg Library

2   The Conflict of Beliefs   30
Karl Jaspers on the Clash of Cultures

3   Between Traditions   46
A Laudatio *for Georg Henrik von Wright*

4   Tracing the Other of History in History   57
On Gershom Scholem's Sabbatai Ṣevi

5   A Master Builder with Hermeneutic Tact   66
The Path of the Philosopher Karl-Otto Apel

6   Israel or Athens: Where does Anamnestic
Reason Belong?   78
Johann Baptist Metz on Unity amidst Multicultural
Plurality

7   Communicative Freedom and Negative Theology   90
Questions for Michael Theunissen

8   The Useful Mole who Ruins the Beautiful Lawn   112
The Lessing Prize for Alexander Kluge

Sources   123

Index   125

Preface

This volume brings together essays and speeches which were written for various occasions. But the themes I addressed as these different opportunities arose may be of more general interest.

In comparison with other philosophers of their generation, the works of Ernst Cassirer and Karl Jaspers have not yet found the echo amongst younger thinkers which they deserve. In the first two chapters I investigate the underlying concerns which gave rise to their philosophies as a whole, with the aim of bringing out the contemporary relevance of their thought. By contrast, memories of the spontaneity of the great story-teller Gershom Scholem are still so vivid that only now are his writings beginning to emerge from the shadow of his unique personality. The central motif of his thinking is closely intertwined with the shimmering figure of the false prophet Sabbatai Ṣevi.

In the remaining essays, I engage with friends and colleagues. Here, too, my conversations are more with the work than with the individual. They can be read as fragments of a history of contemporary philosophy. Alexander Kluge, the great theorizer among writers and film-makers, will forgive me for including him with philosophers, and even theologians.

J.H.
Starnberg, March 1996

1

The Liberating Power of Symbols

Ernst Cassirer's Humanistic Legacy and the Warburg Library

For John Michael Krois, to whose
admonition I shall seek to respond

I

When the University of Hamburg was founded after the First World War, Aby Warburg was able to carry out the plan he had long cherished of making his private library accessible to the public. The library became the focal point of an institute for interdisciplinary research in the human and cultural sciences, where students and visitors were able to work, and where university seminars and public lectures were held. For a small circle of scholars concerned with the study of religion it became an 'organon of humanistic research', as Cassirer was later to put it. In fact, Ernst Cassirer was one of the first to give a lecture there. The following entry can be found in the annual report of the Warburg Library for 1921, written by Fritz Saxl:

This lecture was delivered on 20 April 1995 at the University of Hamburg. The dual occasion was the dedication of the restored Warburg Library building, and the fiftieth anniversary of the death of Ernst Cassirer (who died in New York on 13 April 1945).

Professors Cassirer, Reinhardt, Ritter, Wolff, Junker, and Dr. Panofsky, are now constant users and patrons of the Library. It has even transpired that Prof. Cassirer, in a lecture to the Hamburg Society for the Study of Religion (of which Prof. Warburg was a founder), has taken up ideas which were earlier quite foreign to him, but which he found himself developing as a result of his use of the Library. Prof. Cassirer intends to expand on these ideas in a major work.[1]

The first volume of Cassirer's *Philosophy of Symbolic Forms* did indeed appear two years later. However, the word of thanks to the Library that appears in the preface to the second volume, which is devoted to mythical thought, has a rather different emphasis:

> The first drafts and other preliminary work for this volume were already far advanced when through my call to Hamburg I came into close contact with the Warburg Library. Here I found abundant and almost incomparable material in the field of mythology and general history of religion, and in its arrangement and selection, in the special intellectual stamp which Warburg gave it, it revolved around a unitary central problem related to the basic problem of my own work.[2]

At the beginning of that first lecture in the Library, Cassirer had already spoken in similar terms:

> The questions with which I would like to deal ... had already concerned me over a long period, but now it seemed as though they stood embodied before me. I had an overwhelming feeling that ... this was not merely a collection of books, but a collection of problems. It was not the material of the Library which impressed me in this way; stronger than the impact of the material itself was that made by principles of its organization.[3]

The works which Warburg had collected belonged to many different disciplines, but, in Cassirer's view, they were 'connected to an ideal middle point'. Cassirer rightly emphasizes the independence of his own philosophical development. But the interest which Warburg and Cassirer shared in the symbolic medium of the human mind's forms of expression was the basis of their intellectual affinity.

The books were divided into four sections; and users of the Library were evidently expected to regard the hidden principle of this organization as an invitation to decipher the theory which it implicitly embodied. Viewed in this way, the ordering of the Library encouraged readers to reflect on the theory of symbolization. Indeed, the description of the present state of the Library, which, since 1958, has been housed in Woburn Square in London in an arrangement modelled on the Hamburg original, reads as though inspired by Cassirer's philosophy of the development of symbolic forms. The world of symbolic forms extends from pictorial representation, via verbal expression, to forms of orienting knowledge, which in turn pave the way for practice: 'The library was to lead from the visual image, as the first stage in man's awareness, to language and hence to religion, science and philosophy, all of them products of man's search for orientation, which influence his patterns of behaviour and his actions, the subject matter of history.'[4]

Cassirer also had other reasons to feel at home in the Library. For it was quite astonishingly congenial to his interests and basic approach. (1) Cassirer could not help but be pleased by the role allotted to philosophy; (2) the collection articulated a notion of culture which interested Cassirer from the epistemological angle; (3) furthermore, Cassirer discovered here in all its breadth and variety the literature of the Renaissance, a literature on whose philosophical currents he had worked; (4) and finally, it was not hard for Cassirer to discern a vital motif of his own thinking in the nature of Warburg's interest in the survival of antiquity in modernity.

(1) As Raymond Klibansky reports, the philosophical material in the Library is far from being structured so as to reflect the status of a First Science; rather, philosophy is treated as a discipline amongst others, or is assigned to other disciplines in a foundational role.[5] So, for example, aesthetics is assigned to the history of art, ethics to jurisprudence, and the philosophy of nature to scientific cosmology.

Cassirer could not help but recognize his own conception of philosophy and his own way of working here. The last twentieth-century individual possessed of a universal culture, the author of books on Kant, Goethe and Einstein, Cassirer had acquired expertise in logic and mathematics, the natural and human sciences, and the history of literature, art and religion. He knew that philosophy could only retain its influence through participation in the specialized knowledge of the individual disciplines and through co-operation with them on an equal footing. Cassirer wanted to learn from the sciences. His style was far from that of the transcendental philosopher in search of ultimate foundations, who imagines himself to be always one step ahead of all empirical knowledge. Cassirer mistrusted the imperious attitude of great philosophy, which imagines it has a universal key, despises mundane knowledge, and obstinately burrows into the depths from its narrow patch of ground. Far more than with Heidegger, he agreed with Hegel, who believed that the depths of spirit are only as deep as 'its willingness to expand and immerse itself in intepretation'.[6]

(2) The Warburg Library also encouraged Cassirer's interests in the sense that it represented the object domains which are especially challenging for an epistemology in the Kantian tradition. *The Critique of Pure Reason* was of course intended to explain how natural-scientific knowledge is possible. The historical sciences of culture only developed later, in the course of the nineteenth century. Cassirer realized that transcendental philosophy could not react to this 'fact of the human sciences' in the same way that Kant, in his time, reacted to the fact of Newtonian physics. From a transcendental standpoint, nature is constituted for us at the same time as the object domain of the natural sciences. But the human sciences are concerned with cultural structures, which they find already to hand as pre-scientifically constituted objects. The concept of culture itself can no longer be adequately explained in terms of the constitution of a corresponding domain of scientific objects. Rather, the human sciences are themselves cultural constructs, which they are able to turn

back and reflect on self-referentially, for example, in the form of the history of science. For this reason Cassirer's aim is not that of Dilthey, namely to expand the critique of 'pure' reason into a critique of 'historical' reason. A philosophy of culture is to take the place of a mere expansion of the scope of the theory of knowledge. Passing via the interpretive achievements of the cultural sciences, such a philosophy will reach out to grasp the practical 'understanding of the world', the 'conception of the world' and 'forming of the world' implicit in cultural practice itself, thereby throwing light on the symbolic generation of culture:

> Logic finds itself confronted with entirely new problems, as soon as it tries to look beyond the pure forms of knowledge towards the totality of spiritual forms in which a conception of the world is articulated. Each of them – such as language and myth, religion and art – now reveals itself to be a distinctive organ for the understanding of the world, and also for the creation of ideal worlds, an organ which retains its peculiar rights alongside and over against theoretically elaborated scientific knowledge.[7]

(3)   Right from the beginnings of his scholarly career, Cassirer had embedded epistemological questions in historically specific cultural contexts. Above all, starting with Nicholas of Cusa, he had followed the emergence of the modern conception of nature in the Renaissance. In 1906, in the preface to the first volume of *The Problem of Knowledge in the Philosophy and Science of the Modern Age*, he had declared that the new conception of natural-scientific knowledge had emerged from the confluence of 'a variety of intellectual and cultural forces'; individual philosophical systems should always be related to the 'currents and forces of general intellectual culture'.[8] It was only twenty years later that this programme came to full fruition, when Cassirer approached more or less the same period and the same authors from a somewhat different angle, in order to develop the thesis that it was a new ethical self-conception and a new dynamic feeling for the world which were the

decisive driving forces behind the new conception of
nature embodied in modern physics: 'Anyone unable to
sense within himself the heroic feeling of self-assertion
and of limitless self-expansion will remain blind to the cosmos and its infinity.'[9] This enquiry into *The Individual
and the Cosmos in the Renaissance* is dedicated to Aby Warburg on his sixtieth birthday. Here it becomes clear
what Cassirer owed to his new environment: not so much
the content of his theses as the nature and range of the
historical material which supports them. For now the con-
stellations begin to speak. Cassirer derives philosophical
thoughts from allegories – changes in the philosophical concept of freedom, for example, from the transformations of
the symbol of Fortuna: 'Fortuna with the wheel which seizes
hold of man and spins him around, sometimes raising him
high, sometimes plunging him into the depths, becomes
Fortuna with the sail – and it is no longer she alone who
steers the ship, but rather man himself who (now) sits at the
rudder.'[10]

(4) But above all, in the reflecting mirror of the
assembled books, Cassirer encountered the lifelong concerns
of the learned collector himself. Like many of his contemporaries, who had also been influenced by Nietzsche, Warburg was interested in the return of the archaic in modernity.
He too was concerned with that constellation which proved
such a stimulus for the avant-garde in painting and literature,
psychology and philosophy – Picasso and Braque, Bataille and
Leiris, Freud and Jung, Benjamin and Adorno. Like Benjamin's 'Arcades Project', Warburg's plan for an atlas which
would trace the lines of collective memory remained unful-
filled. Under the keyword 'Mnemosyne' Warburg wanted to
use an ingenious montage of pictorial material to illustrate
the continuing heritage of expressive gestures passed down
from antiquity. In these passionate gestures, tinged with
something phobic and yet aesthetically restrained, he de-
ciphered archaic impulses. The Renaissance interested him
as the stage on which the drama of the re-awakening of pagan
antiquity, an antiquity now purged of its demons, was played
out.

The term 'pagan world' was Warburg's shorthand for that exciting ambivalence of enthralment and emancipation, of chaotic anxiety and orgiastic abandon, which lived on in a sublimated form in the gestures of European enthusiasm: 'More than ever therefore, the Renaissance appears in the *Mnemosyne* as a precious moment of precarious religious equilibrium in which the sources of heathen passions were tapped but still under control.'[11] The force of artistic creation, purged of its demons, clearly had an existential significance for Warburg. The atlas project was to be introduced with the words: 'The conscious creation of distance between oneself and the external world may be called the fundamental act of civilization. Where this gap conditions artistic creativity, this awareness of distance can achieve a lasting social function.'[12]

This idea has a striking resemblance to the fundamental insight on which Cassirer's *Philosophy of Symbolic Forms* also draws. The idea also expresses a practical intention which Cassirer shares, and which he formulates in conceptual terms: the fact that sensory contact with the world is reworked into something meaningful through the use of symbols is the defining feature of human existence, and also constitutes, from a normative standpoint, the basic trait of a properly human mode of being. In other words, the objectifying force of symbolic mediation breaks the animal immediacy of a nature which impacts on the organism from within and without; it thereby creates that distance from the world which makes possible a thoughtful, reflectively controlled reaction to the world on the part of subjects who are able to say 'no'.

Against a *Lebensphilosophie* bent on celebrating the spontaneity of non-alienated life, which at that time had taken on politically virulent forms, Cassirer emphasizes the broken character of our symbolic relation to the world, a relation which is mediated by words and tools. He also stresses the indirectness of a self-relation which forces human beings to make a detour via symbolically generated objectifications in order to return to themselves: 'The world of spirit first emerges when the flow of life no longer simply streams onward... when life, instead... of consuming itself in the act of giving birth, gathers itself together into lasting forms and sets these up outside itself and before itself.'[13] This taking of distance is not, of course, the ascetic activity of a spirit 'hostile to life' (Scheler), which, as 'antagonist of the soul' (Klages), irrupts from without into a 'life blind to ideas'. Rather that intermediate domain of symbolic forms, which the human mind weaves around itself, and through which it interprets itself, arises from a process of 'inner transformation and reversal which life experiences in itself'. This is the fundamental process of symbolization:

> Language and art, myth and theoretical knowledge all contribute to . . . this process of mental distanciation: they are the major stages on the path which leads from the space of what can be grasped and effected, in which the animal lives and within which it remains confined, to the space of sensory experience and thought, to the horizon of mind.[14]

I would now like to show how Cassirer analyses this process of symbolization, which first makes human beings into human beings, as occurring in the field of tension between myth and enlightenment, and how he demonstrates its relevance for a semiotic reformulation of transcendental philosophy (II). We will find that the problems internal to this construction suggest a reading of *The Philosophy of Symbolic Forms* from the standpoint of a theory of civilization – a reading which first sets Cassirer's humanistic inheritance in the correct light. I am not referring here to that obvious inheritance from the Renaissance and the Enlightenment which Cassirer made his own in many learned studies, but the humanistic legacy which his philosophy has bequeathed to us.

II

The most obvious result of the intellectual stimulus which Cassirer received during the twenties, if not from Warburg himself, then from the scholarly discussions of religion in the circle gathered around him in his library, can be found in his important reflections on mythical images and linguistic symbols. The original function of such images and symbols is said to be both the control of affects and the creation of meanings (1). These reflections throw a clearer light on the foundations of a philosophy of symbolic forms, which emerged out of an innovative reception of Humboldt's philosophy of language (2). Even prior to his Hamburg period, Cassirer had employed the philosophy of language as the key to a semiotic reformulation of transcendental philosophy. This allowed him to give the theory of concepts and the problematic of the 'thing-in-itself' a convincing formulation (3).

(1) In 1925 there appeared a treatise on 'Language and Myth' in the series of studies published by Warburg Library, in which Cassirer (drawing primarily on H. Usener's classic work on the formation of religious concepts)[15] dealt with the problem of the names of the gods. Here he analyses the basic process of symbol formation more penetratingly than in the second volume of his masterwork, which had already appeared.[16] Cassirer's aim is to explain how, at the beginning of the process of anthropogenesis, language and myth apparently emerge simultaneously from 'the same basic act of mental processing, of the concentration and intensification of simple sensory intuition'. Language and myth are 'two diverse shoots from the same parent stem, the same impulse of symbolic formulation',[17] but, in the course of their differentiation into a world of images and a linguistic world, they go in opposite directions. Mythical images are a condensation of individual, meaning-laden impressions, which remain bound to their original context, whereas in the medium of language individual cases are generalized into exemplary cases or into an articulated whole.

Acts of symbolization are distinguished by the fact that they break open environments shaped by the peculiarities of a particular species. This they do by transforming fluctuating sense impressions into semantic meanings and fixing them in such a way that the human mind can reproduce the

impressions in memory and preserve them. Thereby the
temporal dimensions of past and future are also opened up
to the human mind. Animal awareness of time stands under
the dominance of the present:

> the past is preserved only in darkness, the future is not raised
> to the level of an image, as something which can be anticip-
> ated. It is the symbolic expression which first creates the
> possibility of looking backward and looking forward. . . . What
> occurred in the past, now separated out from the totality of
> representations, no longer passes away, once the sounds of
> language have placed their seal upon it and given it a certain
> stamp.[18]

In creating meanings which remain self-identical, symbolization creates a medium for thoughts which can transcend the
temporal stream of consciousness.

Symbolic form is thus originally generated by a stylizing
force, which condenses the dramatic impact of experiences.
Here Cassirer makes use of Usener's theory of 'momentary
gods' to account for symbolic condensation as a response to
the exciting ambivalence of meaning-laden experiences.
Think of a hill protecting someone from pursuit, the water
which saves a person dying of thirst, a sudden noise or wild
animal which pounces on the solitary individual – of any
situation or object which both repels and allures, which
both arouses horror and releases tension, which tears the
soul back and forth between terror and attraction. Such
compressed, highly significant experiences, which are the
focus of an isolating attention, can congeal into a mythical
image, can be semanticized and thereby spellbound, given
fixity by a divine name which makes it possible to recall and
control them. Through the symbolic transformation of sense
experience into meaning, affective tension is both discharged
and stabilized. Cassirer speaks of an almost violent separation
and isolation of the strong impression: 'only when this split-
ting off succeeds, when intuition is compressed into a single
point and apparently reduced to it, does a mythical or linguistic structure result, only then can the word or the

momentary god emerge.'[19] Of course, not just any objective content of intuition can be condensed into the meaning of a symbol, but only those contents of experience which are affectively relevant for a being which can hope and suffer, which has interests and concerns. This explains the 'passionate' character which Warburg discovered in primordial expressive gestures.

Yet if the process of symbolization amounted to no more than the spell-binding and condensing power to objectify individual, meaning-laden experiences in mythical form, then the subject would remain caught in a world of images. The dialectical character of symbolization consists in the fact that it also points in the opposite direction, towards an exemplary generalization and comprehensive ordering of the fixed expressions within an articulated whole:

> As soon as the spark has leapt across, as soon as the tension and the affect of the moment have been discharged in a word or in a mythical image, then a reversal can start to occur with the mind.... Now a process of objectification can begin which advances ever further. As the activity of human beings extends over an ever wider area, so a progressive subdivision and ever more precise articulation of both the mythical and the linguistic world is achieved.[20]

The spell-binding tendency that congeals intense experiences in specific forms is counteracted by the conceptualizing tendency, which points towards generalization and specification.

Although language and myth have a common root in the stratum of metaphorical expression, they are differentiated from each other along the axes of the production of a plenitude of meaning conveyed by images, on the one hand, and the logical disclosure of a categorially articulated world, on the other. Language, which becomes the vehicle of thought, conceals a logical power and 'free ideality' which are alien to myth. The mythical image stands in for the 'obscure plenitude of being' which only propositional discourse can release, by giving it a 'linguistically accessible articulation'. Myth and language are a central theme of the philosophy of symbolic forms because the basic concept of symbolization entwines two meaning-creating functions: expression and concept. Expression transforms forceful sense impressions into meaningful elements, individual mythical images, which are able to stabilize affective responses; concepts articulate a view of the world as a whole. In his analysis of the expressive function, which is unmistakeably inspired by myth, Cassirer was stimulated by the discussions in Warburg's circle. But, as regards the linguistic function of world-disclosure, Cassirer had already learned much from Humboldt prior to his arrival in Hamburg. The insights drawn from the study of religion helped to deepen a conception which ultimately derived from Cassirer's genuine insights in the domain of the philosophy of language.

(2) Cassirer's original achievement consists in a semiotic transformation of Kantian transcendental philosophy. This achievement deserves to stand side by side with the transcendental turn which Wittgenstein – in his *Tractatus Logico-Philosophicus* – introduced into Fregean semantics at around the same time. Cassirer was the first to perceive the paradigmatic significance of Humboldt's philosophy of language; and he thus prepared the way for my generation, the post-war generation, to take up the 'linguitic turn' in analytical philosophy and integrate it with the native tradition of hermeneutic philosophy. The three decisive steps are recorded in a brilliant essay on 'The Kantian Element in Wilhelm von Humboldt's Philosophy of Language': (a) a turning away from the traditional nomination theory of language; (b) a structuralist overcoming of the Kantian dualism of freedom and necessity; and (c) a new interpretation of synthesis and objectification in terms of the theory of symbols.

(a) In the philosophical tradition language was always analysed in accordance with a model of naming or designation: we give names to represented objects, and thereby construct a system of markers which facilitates thinking and makes possible communication about thoughts and ideas. But language, regarded as a medium which is only subsequently introduced between the representing subject and the world of represented objects, also falls under suspicion as a source of confusion. In order to grasp reality as it truly is, we must pull aside the curtain of words which conceals being.[21] By contrast, Humboldt conceives of language in a way which endows it with a disclosing function. Language now becomes a productive force, through which the world is initially revealed to the knowing subject: 'Languages are... not in fact means of representing a truth which is already known, but rather means of discovering what was previously unknown.'[22] Naturally, the reference to existing or represented objects is an important function of language; but its distinctive productive achievement consists in the conceptual articulation of a world of possible states of affairs. The analysis of language should not, therefore, take its bearings from the role of names or individual words, but from the structure of propositions. In this context propositions appear not as the 'copy of a meaning which is already fixed and given in the consciousness of the speaker', but as 'vehicles for the conferring of meaning'. In other words, it is only grammatical form which gives structure to states of affairs:

> What is objective [is] not the given, but that which has to be won through effort, not what is determinate in itself, but that which is to be determined. Since this basic process of determination, seen from a linguistic standpoint, occurs in propositions, Humboldt's philosophy of language emphasizes the primacy of the proposition over the word, just as Kant's transcendental logic emphasized the primacy of the judgement over the concept.[23]

Guided by the model of transcendental logic, Humboldt describes the productivity of language as a world-projecting spontaneity. He takes from Kant the notion of the transcendental production of a categorially structured world of objects of possible experience, in order to explain the meaning-conferring function of language. The spontaneous process of world constitution is thus transferred from the transcendental subject to a natural language employed by empirical subjects; the constitution of a domain of objects is similarly transformed into the grammatical pre-structuring of a linguistically articulated world. The 'inner form of language' is the initial shaper of a 'view' of the world as a whole. Whatever the members of a linguistic community may encounter in the world is accessible only via the linguistic forms of a possible shared understanding concerning such experiences.

(b) Of course, Cassirer is not interested simply in this new conception of language. Above all, he is concerned to investigate how transcendental philosophy itself alters in the course of its linguistic transformation, with the aim of making the transformed transcendental approach also fruitful for the analysis of non-linguistic phenomena. Language is no longer limited to an instrumental role, but acquires a constitutive status, so that its productive energies appear to unfold a life of their own. Hence sign and meaning can no longer be assigned – as on the mentalistic model – to two different spheres, as if the representing subject connected a pre-existing immaterial idea with a material substrate. Rather the speaking subject herself now becomes a link in the process whereby symbolically structured forms of life and thought are maintained and renewed. The symbolic medium has a structure which embraces both the internal and the external: 'The world of the subject and that of the object are no longer opposed to each other as two halves of absolute being, rather it is one and the same cycle of intellectual functions which enables us...to achieve both the separation and reciprocal connection [of subject and object].'[24]

The intersubjectively shared domain of language, which is both *energeia* and *ergon*, creative rule and creation, possesses a distinctive kind of objectivity: language puts its stamp on the awareness of speaking subjects and also provides them with a medium for the expression of their own experiences: 'Language is effective and autonomous from the objective point of view precisely to the extent that it is exploited and

dependent from the subjective standpoint.'[25] The contraven-
tion of grammatical rules reveals the stubborn reality of
language, over which no one can claim control as if it
were private property; on the other hand, language does
not imprison subjects, but endows them with powers
of free productivity, which even include the possibility of
revising and creatively renewing the vocabulary of world-
disclosure.

   This notion of language implies more than just a new
linguistic theory. By commandeering Kant's notion of
the transcendental, so to speak, and transforming the
world-constituting activity of the knowing subject into the
world-disclosing function of the trans-subjective form of
language, it explodes the architectonic of the philosophy of
consciousness as a whole. Symbolic form overcomes the
opposition of subject and object. Linguistic productivity is
immune to dualism both from a practical and a theoretical
standpoint. On the one hand it is a 'true creation of
the mind', and yet – since it is not at the disposition of the
individual – it appears to be a 'product of nature'. Cassirer
concludes: 'Thus the basic opposition which dominates the
entire systematics of Kant's thought seems inadequate...
when it comes to defining the specificity of the domain of
language as a product of the mind.'[26] In short, the
new conception of language provides the basis for a new
paradigm.

   (c) At the same time, Cassirer seems to have underes-
timated the scope of these innovations. He retains an
epistemological standpoint in the sense that he interprets
linguistic world-disclosure on the model of the transcendental constitution of objects of possible experience. He assimilates Humboldt's linguistic articulation of the world to
Kant's constitution of a domain of objects of possible experience. He reduces both to the common denominator of the
categorial articulation of a symbolically generated world.
Relying on an analogy with categorial synthesis, which first
endows the manifold of sense impressions with the unity of
the objective experience of things, he also understands the
function of linguistic form in terms of 'objectification'. In

so doing, he exploits the ambivalence of the expression 'objectification'; for we also use this term to describe the process of externalization which characterizes the sensuous, symbolic embodiment of an intellectual content: 'What Kant describes as the activity of judgement is only made possible in the concrete life of the mind by the mediating intervention of language, as Humboldt makes clear. Objectification in thought must pass via objectification in the sounds of language.'[27] This interpretation is the direct descendant of the theory of concepts which Cassirer had already developed by 1910.[28] In addition, it allows for an elegant reading of Cohen's conjuring away of the 'thing-in-itself'.[29]

(3) Ever since Plato, conceptual systems have been differentiated logically in terms of genus and species. However, the suggestive image of the tree diagram encouraged the false assumption that concepts were the copies of structures, or of systems of essential connections. By contrast with this copying function, Cassirer stresses the disclosive function of conceptual elaboration: concepts are constructively generated viewpoints, which allow us to bring a disorderly mass of perceptual or intellectual elements into connection. Along with such points of reference for ordering, concepts create new possibilities of comparison, which allow ever new relations between like and unlike to emerge. After his semiotic turn, Cassirer explains this perspective-generating character of conceptual elaboration with the help of the symbolic function (and comments on it with the help – for example – of Frege's and Russell's analysis of propositional functions[30]). In this way he integrates Kant's functionalistic theory of concepts with the idea, borrowed from the theory of language, that conceptual synthesis is dependent on the unifying force of signs. The externalizing, object-constituting force of symbolic systems finds expression in the creative spontaneity of conceptual articulation.

Viewed from this perspective, the awkward *Ding-an-sich* also disappears – a notion which suggests that the understanding, in its categorizing function, stamps its forms on material which is given 'in itself'. The sense impressions which call forth the act of symbolization are not ontically given, but rather a limit quantity which we are obliged to postulate. As soon as form-giving power is transferred from the knowing subject to symbolic representation itself, it becomes clear that the difference between symbolic form and that which can only be presented in the medium of symbolic form should not be hypostatized into an ontic distinction. Represented objects can only come into existence within the horizon opened by the primordial creative power of symbolic representation. Outside of the symbolically grounded relation between a linguistic expression and what it affirms, such an attribution of existence is strictly meaningless.

III

Thus mythology and the theory of language are the two sources on which Cassirer draws in clarifying the nature of symbolization, and thereby the basis of a philosophy designed to expand the critique of knowledge into a critique of culture in general. I would like first of all to take a closer look at the construction of this theory, and indicate the tensions between two theses. On the one hand, Cassirer insists on the equal rights of equiprimordial symbolic worlds, but, on the other hand, he follows the traces of a tendency towards emancipation which is built into cultural development (1). I will then mention some difficulties which result from the characteristic style of epistemological inquiry which Cassirer retains (2). Only when we abandon these perspectives and read the philosophy of symbolic forms as a theory of the civilizing process does its true humanistic content become apparent. This intention repeatedly inspired Cassirer whenever he took a stand against the growing barbarity of a highly cultured nation. This he did as rector of this university, as a politically conscious citizen of the Weimar Republic, as a persecuted emigrant, and as a resolutely engaged contemporary, arguing in a Kantian spirit – with increasing despair, to be sure, but never so as to dishearten (3).

(1)   As we have seen, Cassirer understands the symbolizing process as an interplay of contrary tendencies. The world of symbolic meanings arises on the one hand from the production of a plenitude of meaningful images, and on the other from the logical disclosure of categorially articulated domains of experience. Of course, these opposing and yet interwoven tendencies are not both equally at work in all symbolic forms. Where the spellbinding tendency causes the sense impression to congeal into a pictorial form, the expressive function has the upper hand; where the tendency towards conceptual elaboration and abstract articulation is preponderant, then the signifying function dominates; where the two tendencies are in equilibrium, the representational function comes to the fore. Once more Cassirer makes reference to everyday language in order to introduce these three functions.

Language 'in the phase of sensuous expression' is saturated with metaphor, and generally characterized by gestures and corporeal expressions, excited sounds and demonstrative movements. Here signs are still fused with the designated object and its significance. Analogical language fulfils functions of expression. Language is able to take over representational functions only when it can be related to things in an objectifying way via expressions which are connected with specific situations, and yet independent of any determinate context. This propositionally differentiated language is language in its usual state of embeddedness in the lifeworld; its serves to orient us in our everyday practice, which is bound up with our sense experience. Only the language of the theoretical sciences, which serves specialized cognitive purposes, can emancipate itself from these ties. It fulfils signifying functions in the sense in which Fregean 'thoughts' are freed from their contexts of utterance and reflect only abstract patterns, ultimately in mathematical terms.

The functions of sensuous expression, perceptual representation and pure meaning thus correspond to the stages of a progressive decontextualization and objectification. However, this pull towards abstraction is revealed not only in language, but in all symbolic worlds. Even the mythical form of thought turns against its own principle of pictorial condensation in the form of monotheistic religions hostile to images. Naturally, the rituals and language of these highly developed religions cannot free themselves entirely from their mythical foundations without exploding their distinctive symbolic form, and thereby losing the essential quality of the sacred. On the other hand, in general there are elective affinities between myth and the expressive function, language and the representational function, and science and the signifying function. This explains why language occupies a position between myth and logos.

Processes of abstraction, which occur both within individual symbolic forms and between them, bring about an increase of freedom for the subjects caught up in them. But the exorcism of demons and liberation from the violence of primaeval mythic powers has a price: 'finally [in science] nothing seems to remain of the concrete contents of intuition and feeling, of the living body, except the bare skeleton.' Only art promises a happy equilibrium between freedom and abstraction:

> there is one domain of spirit in which the word not only retains its original power as an image, but also experiences a sensuous and spiritual rebirth. This regeneration occurs when it is shaped into an artistic form of expression. Here the fullness of life is returned to it: but this is no longer a mythically bound life, but rather an aesthetically liberated one.[31]

In this way Cassirer introduces the four worlds of myth, language, art and science which form the backbone of the 'philosophy of symbolic forms'. The manner in which they are introduced immediately raises the delicate question of the evaluation of symbolic forms. It is interesting to find that this question can be discounted only as long as the different spheres of spirit can be regarded, from an epistemological standpoint, as so many 'worlds', in which

spirit is simultaneously objectivated. As long as Cassirer
still remains tied, despite everything, to his neo-Kantian
beginnings, and interprets the symbolic forms as strategies
of objectification, then myth, language and art each
create their own form-specific object domains, just like the
mathematical natural sciences. In these object domains
the familiar categories of space, time, substance and causality
are simply transformed in accordance with different modalities:

> Thus each of them creates its own distinctive symbolic
> formations, which are not of the same kind as intellectual
> symbols, but nevertheless of equal rank. None of these for-
> mations can be simply absorbed by another or derived from
> another, but rather each of them refers to a specific mode of
> mental apprehension, within and through which it constitu-
> tes its own dimension of the 'real'.[32]

This perspectivism suggests a pluralism of worlds, one to
which others could be added. Occasionally Cassirer dealt
with technology as a further symbolic form. He also men-
tions 'law and morality, the basic forms of community and
those of the state'. From the standpoint of validity, symbolic
forms stand side by side with equal rights, even though myth
has a certain priority from the genetic viewpoint: 'they do
not appear immediately as separate . . . forms, but rather all
gradually free themselves from the common originating
ground of myth.'[33]

(2) This perspectivism runs up against familiar
objections. In Cassirer's case it conjures up yet again the
problematic of the 'thing-in-itself', which he assumed he
had overcome. Long ago Konrad Marc-Wogau made this
the basis of his critique, in a review to which Cassirer
responded in a rather unconvincing way.[34] Marc-Wogau
refers to an example which Cassirer employs many times,
according to which we can interpret the same line in different ways, depending on which symbolic form takes the leading role. We can see it as an ornament or a phenomenon of
style, or as the symbol of a religious cult, or as a sine curve,

and so forth.[35] It is clear that the identity of the sense impression, as the point of reference of the different interpretations, can only be maintained when this impression is endowed with the significance of a reality 'in itself', independent of all interpretations. But Cassirer would then have to concede precisely that metaphysical separation of matter and form which he rightly wishes to avoid because of its contradictory consequences. On the other hand, he cannot give up on the premiss that there is a unity of reality within the multiplicity of perspectives. For as long as symbolic forms alone provide objectivity and validity, then they must all refer to the same reality. Today we would formulate the problem by saying that Cassirer cannot assert both of the following at the same time: that the different symbolic languages are incommensurable, and that they can nevertheless be at least partially translated into one another.

The question of commensurability becomes pressing when one realizes that the semiotic turn not only does away with the reference point of an objective world, but also the transcendental subject beyond the world. As soon as the transcendental operations are transferred to different systems of symbols, then the transcendental subject loses its place beyond the empirical world. It loses its pure intelligibility and autonomy. It is drawn, along with its symbolic embodiments, into the process of history, and fragmented into a pluralism of languages and cultures. This de-transcendentalization would result in the identity of reason itself being dissolved into a multiplicity of contexts, were there no translation mechanism built into symbolic languages themselves, making possible communication across the frontiers between them. As long as Cassirer holds onto the perspective of the theory of knowledge, he has to regard the unity of reason as anchored in an extramundane mind, which objectifies itself in the various symbolic forms:

> The forms in which life externalizes itself and thanks to which it takes on an 'objective' shape, signify resistance to life, yet they also represent its indispensable support ... only

an orientation towards the externality of forms and symbols, as opposed to that of things, offers a path along which pure subjectivity can find itself.[36]

But with such reflections Cassirer steps beyond the limits of a critical epistemology in the direction of objective ideal- ism. This can already be seen from the fact that he can no longer indicate the place from which he himself is speaking. Philosophy, which analyses all symbolic languages, lacks a language of its own. For a symbolic form capable of raising itself above all other symbolic forms would be paradoxical in terms of Cassirer's own assumptions.

Heidegger correctly identified this weakness in his famous controversy with Cassirer at Davos:

> One could say that for Cassirer the terminus ad quem is the whole of a philosophy of culture in the sense of an elucida- tion of the wholeness of the forms of the shaping conscious- ness. For Cassirer the terminus a quo is utterly problematical ... Cassirer's point is to emphasize the various forms of the shaping in order, with a view to these shapings, subsequently to point out a certain dimension of the shaping powers themselves.[37]

Heidegger means to suggest, of course, that he has led us into this fundamental dimension, which remains unexplained in Cassirer, with his analysis of being-in-the-world in *Being and Time*. But it is worth noting that Cassirer, on the basis of his reception of Humboldt, had already long since achieved the turn towards a pragmatics of language which still lay in the future for Heidegger. Ironically, he could therefore have taken account of Heidegger's warning, which seems to me justified, better than Heidegger himself. But this would have required a step which Cassirer was unwilling to take: he would have had to transform the heuristic priority which the transcendental analysis of language and of the linguistic- ally constituted lifeworld does in fact enjoy in his researches[38] into a systematic priority. He would have had to give language and the lifeworld a central position in the construction of symbolic forms.

With this step Cassirer could have overcome his epistemologically constricted vision, and resolved the conflict between the perspectivism of equiprimordial worlds, on the one hand, and the emancipatory power of symbolic shaping, on the other, which dogs his philosophy of symbolic forms. The question of the evaluation of symbolic forms remained open, and the normative foundations remained entirely unclear. This may be the systematic reason why the controversy in Davos did not touch on the real crux of the dispute. The conflict between Cassirer and Heidegger, which extended into the political domain, was not played out. The opposition between the decent, cultured spirit of a cosmopolitan humanism, and that fatal rhetoric set on throwing man back onto the 'hardness of his fate', was reflected only in a contrast of gestures and mentalities.

(3) During this period Cassirer enjoyed a level of academic fame which he never achieved again in Germany after his emigration. He is one of those few brave exceptions in the realm of the German mandarins who defended the Weimar Republic against its cultured despisers. When Cassirer took a stand on matters of public concern he made no attempt to conceal his fundamental normative convictions. In 1928, a year before his encounter with Heidegger, Cassirer had made an official speech on Constitution Day. In this speech he sketched with bold strokes the origins of human rights and democracy in the tradition of rational law, with the aim of bringing home a single thought to his public: 'the idea of a republican constitution is in no sense a stranger, let alone an alien intruder, in the overall context of the history of German thought and culture. Rather, it grew out of this very ground, and was nourished by its most authentic forces, the forces of Idealist philosophy.'[39]

Cassirer appealed repeatedly to Kant's theory of law. Time and again he explained the internal connection between individualism on the one hand, and universalism on the other. The understated pathos of the rational moral

law gives Cassirer's writings an unmistakeable profile. It is
therefore all the more surprising that the normative shapes of
spirit, namely law and morality, are often mentioned but
have no explicit place in the systematic construction of the
symbolic forms. Not even the sole treatise of any size on this
theme, a study of the philosophy of Axel Hagerström which
was written in exile in Sweden,[40] contains more than a
defence of the deontological approach against non-cognitivist
conceptions of morality. Cassirer obviously believed that the
philosophy of symbolic forms as such had a moral-practical
content, which rendered the working out of an independent
ethics superfluous. But this philosophy only offers such a
content when it is no longer viewed as theory of knowledge
applicable to the whole of culture, and is seen as a theory of
the civilizing process. This process has also to be understood
humanistically, as a movement towards increasing civility.
This leads us back to the key notion of symbolization
which Cassirer shares with Warburg.

In that 'state of awareness which hovers between grasping
and being grasped' described by Warburg, Cassirer recognized the specific characteristic of a mentality shaped by
symbols. Mind only makes contact with its environment in
a mediated way. The position of human beings in the world is
defined by a form-giving power which transforms sense
impressions into meaningful structures. Human beings master the forces of nature which rush in upon them through
symbols which spring from the productive imagination. Thus
they gain a distance from the immediate pressure of nature.
Of course, they pay for this emancipation with their mental
dependence on a semanticized nature, which returns in the
spellbinding force of mythical images. That first act of
distantiation must therefore be repeated in the course
of cultural development. The break with first nature is
continued in the second, symbolically generated nature –
with the opening up of symbolic worlds, in fact. As we
have seen, this objectification is made possible by the
world-disclosing logos of language. In the process of anthropogenesis, symbolic mediation takes on ever more complex
forms and guides the contact with nature onto ever more

indirect paths. Through this process, distance, freedom and reflexivity increase, but they exact a price: 'When human beings dare to release themselves from the the tutelage of nature, and . . . to rely on their own willing and thinking, they also give up all the benefits which proximity to nature implied.'[41]

Cassirer makes no assumptions about a progressive logic of cultural development. Within each sphere there occurs the same dialectic, one in which independence increases at the cost of new dependencies. And no symbolic form, not even that of myth, loses its peculiar rights in favour of another sphere. But at the same time, in the dynamic of symbolization which drives the process of civilization forward, there is also an element which promotes increasingly civilized behaviour: 'It seems to be the fundamental feature of all human existence that human beings are not entirely absorbed by the plethora of external impressions, rather they limit this plenitude by stamping a particular form on it. In the last analysis this form comes from themselves as thinking, feeling, willing subjects.'[42] In the symbolic constitution of human existence and in the symbolic mediation of our life activity the path towards a humane conduct of life is already anticipated. The symbol-using animal finds itself caught up in cultural processes which have a compass built into them. For this reason, Cassirer refuses to regard the eighteenth century's ideal of humanity as no more than an ethical ideal. What the classics once sought 'in the name of humanity' does not 'lie within the limits of ethical form'. A theory which can illuminate the humane meaning of civilization, along with the process of symbolization as such, has already essentially achieved what can be expected of a philosophical ethics.

And yet normatively significant cultural processes are constantly exposed to the danger of collapse. It is well known that Cassirer devoted his last book to the analysis of contemporary totalitarianism.[43] He perceives the political practice of the Nazis as an ominous fusion of myth and technology: fascist mobilization succeeds by employing modern techniques of mass communication in the service of the revival of mythical forms of thought. It is worth noting that Cassirer trusts religious far more than scientific enlightenment as a counter-force to the violence of political myths – he relies on the confinement of myth within its own proper sphere, which was long ago achieved by monotheism. 'Judaism and the Modern Political Myths' is the title of one of Cassirer's last essays. It is a moving document of German-Jewish thought. Of course, the fact that this document was written not in German but in English, and indeed in exile, confirms that sceptical gaze which Gershom Scholem turned on the fragile symbiosis of German-Jewish culture. This essay dating from 1944 ends with the words:

> No Jew can and will ever overcome the terrible ordeal of these last years ... Yet amidst all these horrors and miseries there is, at least, one relief ... What the modern Jew had to defend ... was not only his physical existence or the preservation of the Jewish race. Much more was at stake. We had to represent all those ethical ideals that had been brought into being by Judaism and found their way into general human culture, into the life of all civilized nations. And here we stand on firm ground ... If Judaism has contributed to breaking the power of the modern political myths, it has done its duty, having once more fulfilled its historical and religious mission.[44]

The humanistic legacy which Cassirer bequeaths to us through his philosophy consists not least in sensitizing us to the fake primordiality of political myths. Cassirer makes us wary of the intellectual celebration of archaic origins, which is widespread today, as in the 1930s. Political myths return because they are hybrid phenomena. They draw on the exotic substance of a stratum of mythical images which is anchored in the symbolic constitution of human existence itself. The haunting of these satyr songs can only be dispelled by an enlightenment which is conscious of the dialectical nature of symbolization. Enlightenment must be able to acknowledge its own roots in the first phobic stirrings of the civilizing process.

Notes

1 T. von Stockhausen, *Die Kulturwissenschaftliche Bibliothek Warburg* (Hamburg: Dölling and Galitz, 1992), p. 127.

2 E. Cassirer, *The Philosophy of Symbolic Forms Volume Two: Mythical Thought*, tr. Ralph Manheim (New Haven and London: Yale University Press, 1955), p. xviii.

3 E. Cassirer, 'Der Begriff der symbolischen Form im Aufbau der Geisteswissenschaften' (1921/22), in *Wesen und Wirkung des Symbolbegriffs* (Darmstadt: WBG, 1956), p. 171.

4 *Die Kulturwissenschaftliche Bibliothek Warburg*, p. 88.

5 Ibid., p. 89.

6 *Wesen und Wirkung des Symbolbegriffs*, p. 200.

7 E. Cassirer, 'Die Begriffsform im mythischen Denken', in *Wesen und Wirkung des Symbolbegriffs*, p. 7.

8 E. Cassirer, *Das Erkenntnisproblem in der Philosophie der Neuzeit*, vol. 1 (1906) (Darmstadt: WBG, 1971), p. viii. Cassirer adds in a vein which is far from neo-Kantian: 'Here the deceptive notion of the "absolute" disappears of its own accord, as soon as we take the first steps. Once we regard the preconditions of science as having come into existence, then we also recognize them as creations of thought. By seeing through their historical relativity and their conditioned status, we open up the prospect of their irresistible progress and ever-renewed productivity' (p. vi).

9 E. Cassirer, *Individuum und Kosmos in der Philosophie der Renaissance* (Leipzig: Studien der Bibliothek Warburg, vol. 10, 1927), p. 142.

10 Ibid., p. 81.

11 E. H. Gombrich, *Aby Warburg: An Intellectual Biography* (London: The Warburg Institute, University of London, 1970), p. 296. See also W. Sauerländer, 'Rescuing the Past', *New York Review of Books*, March 1988, pp. 19–22.

12 Cited in *Aby Warburg*, p. 288.

13 E. Cassirer, *Geist und Leben*, ed. Ernst W. Orth (Leipzig: Reclam, 1993), pp. 45ff.

14 Ibid., p. 51.

15 Hermann Usener, *Götternamen* (Bonn: Friedrich Cohen, 1896).

16 *Philosophie der symbolischen Formen*, vol. 2.

17 Ernst Cassirer, *Language and Myth*, tr. Suzanne K. Langer (New York and London: Harper and Brothers, 1946), p. 88.

18 *Wesen und Wirkung des Symbolbegriffs*, p. 107.

19 Ibid., p. 123.

20 Ibid., p. 105.

21 E. Cassirer, 'Die Kantische Element in Wilhelm von Humboldts Sprachphilosophie' (1923), in *Geist und Leben*, p. 246.

22 *Geist und Leben*, p. 260.

23 Ibid., p. 258.

24 Ibid., pp. 270ff.

25 Ibid., p. 261.

26 Ibid., p. 239.

27 Ibid., p. 256.

28 E. Cassirer, *Substanzbegriff und Funktionsbegriff* (Berlin: B. Cassirer, 1910).

29 *Das Erkenntnisproblem*, vol. 2 (1922) (Darmstadt: WBG, 1971), pp. 733–62.

30 E. Cassirer, The *Philosophy of Symbolic Forms Volume Three: The Phenomenology of Knowledge*, tr. Ralph Mannheim (New Haven and London: Yale University Press, 1957), p. 294 (trans. altered by PD).

31 *Wesen und Wirkung*, p. 157.

32 E. Cassirer, *The Philosophy of Symbolic Forms Volume One: Language*, tr. Ralph Mannheim (New Haven and London: Yale University Press, 1955), p. 78 (trans. altered by PD).

33 *Wesen und Wirkung*, p. 157.

34 E. Cassirer, 'Zur Logik des Symbolbegriffs', in ibid., pp. 203–30.

35 E. Cassirer, 'Das Symbolproblem und seine Stellung in der Philosophie', in John M. Krois and Ernst w. Orth, eds, *Symbol, Technik, Sprache* (Hamburg: Felix Meiner, 1985), pp. 5ff.

36 *The Philosophy of Symbolic Forms Volume Three*, p. 40 (trans. altered by PD).

37 'Davos Disputation between Ernst Cassirer and Martin Heidegger', appendix II in M. Heidegger, *Kant and the Problem of Metaphysics* (Bloomington and Indianapolis: Indiana University Press, 1990), pp. 180–1.

38 E. Cassirer, 'Die Sprache und der Aufbau der Gegenstandswelt' (1932–3), in *Symbol, Technik, Sprache*, pp. 121–51.

39 E. Cassirer, *Die Idee der Republikanischen Verfassung* (Hamburg: Friederichsen, de Gruyter & Co., 1929), p. 31.

40 E. Cassirer, *Axel Hagerström* (Göteborg: Göteborgs Högskolas årsskrift, no. 1, 1939).
41 *Symbol, Technik, Sprache*, p. 74.
42 E. Cassirer, *Naturalistische und humanistische Begründung der Kulturphilosophie* (Göteborg: Wettergren & Kerber, 1939).
43 E. Cassirer, *The Myth of the State* (New Haven: Yale University Press, 1946).
44 E. Cassirer, 'Judaism and the Modern Political Myths', *Contemporary Jewish Record*, no. 7, 1944, p. 126.

2

The Conflict of Beliefs

Karl Jaspers on the Clash of Cultures

I

Today the struggle between different faiths which Weber described in his famous diagnosis of the times has acquired the directly political form of a clash of cultures. This current world situation lends surprising relevance to a theme which is of central importance in the philosophy of Karl Jaspers. In the foreword to a work written at the end of his life, *Philosophical Faith in the Face of Revelation*, which appeared in 1962, Jaspers states:

> Today we are in search of the basis on which human beings from all the various religious traditions could encounter each other in a meaningful way across the entire world, ready to re-appropriate, purify and transform their own historical traditions, but not to abandon them. Such common ground for the (plurality of) faiths could only be clarity of thought, truthfulness and a shared basic knowledge. Only these (three elements) would permit that boundless communication in which the wellsprings of faith could draw each other closer, by virtue of their essential commitment.[1]

The programme on which the United Nations was founded after the catastrophes of the Second World War promised the

Acceptance speech on the occasion of the award of the Karl Jaspers Prize of the Town and University of Heidelberg on 26 September 1995.

international triumph of human rights and democracy. This politics of human rights has aroused the suspicion that it is merely a veil for the hegemonic ambitions and naked predominance of Western culture. Since the collapse of the Soviet empire and the end of a polarization of the world which seemed to reflect a conflict of basic social policies, conflicts are increasingly defined from a cultural standpoint. They are viewed as conflicts of peoples and cultures whose self-understanding has been shaped by the traditions of opposing world religions. In this situation, we Europeans are faced with the task of achieving an intercultural understanding between the world of Islam and the Judaeo-Christian West.

Jaspers is convinced that philosophy can foster a way of thinking which could secure religious peace for a second time – this time on a worldwide basis. He even puts his own philosophical work at the service of a form of communication which might at least tame the tension between antagonistic beliefs and transform it into a discursive conflict, even if it cannot entirely dissolve it. A discordant tolerance could then take the place of armed brutality: 'In the real world the assertion of our own existence demands ... a real struggle against alien gods and demons. In order to contain this struggle ... rational beings seek to draw all means of communication from insight into our basic human situation.'[2] Thus, philosophically mediated insight into the essential situation of human beings is supposed to overcome the will to destruction through a will to communication. 'Basic philosophical knowledge' is intended to foster a pacifying mode of communication. This would reconcile those who are locked in intellectual struggle. It would link together parties who are both in conflict with and learning from each other, without erasing legitimate oppositions.

Jaspers also regarded his conception, as Gadamer later regarded his philosophical hermeneutics, as a reponse to the aporias of an unrestrained historicism. Existential communication was intended to foster mutual understanding between alien traditions and forms of life, but not at the cost of an apparently selfless, but normatively blind empathy with the other. Jaspers takes the sincerity of a self-conscious conduct of life to be the ethical criterion which allows us to assess the existential viability of a form of belief. Parties to a communicative dispute must allow themselves to be guided by the 'hope for unanimity', but they may hold fast to existentially tried and tested convictions, without becoming inflexible about them. 'Unanimity', in this context, suggests a form of agreement which is not to be found at the level of propositional content. But if the consensus does not extend to *contents* of belief, but only to the authentic way in which these contents are made manifest in the conduct of life, how can the basis for a possible unification be understood?

In his early years Jaspers was marked by the aristocratic heritage of Platonism. He based the unanimity at which he aimed on the mutual respect with which great prophets and thinkers, each drawing on his own primordial sources, are able to regard each other. This approach can still be detected in *The Great Philosophers*,[3] among whom Jaspers counts not only Socrates, but also Buddha, Confucius and Jesus, who were founding figures of the great epochal turn in human history. They broke the spell of mythical thought with their words and deeds, and triggered the process of disenchantment which has continued right up until the modern period. But historical experiences later transformed the liberal conservative into a convinced democrat (even though Jaspers did not abandon his reservations concerning party-political democracy, any more than did his pupil Hannah Arendt). Of course it cannot be taken for granted that an approach based on the notion of a spiritual elite can be reconciled with Jaspers' new egalitarian premises. Morally grounded equal respect for each individual is due to the person as such, and indeed independently of whether we *value* her way of life and the traditions on which it draws.

Jaspers bases his central concept of existential communication on the model of the friendly polemics between great philosophers (just as he himself argued polemically with Schelling, for example[4]). I would like to pursue the question of whether this form of communication is appropriate as a model for the intercultural understanding which is urgently needed today for political reasons. I will first outline the current state of the discussion on this issue (II), to provide a background which will bring Jaspers's conception into relief (III). With a sidelong glance at John Rawls (IV) I shall propose, against Jaspers the philosopher of existence, that the 'conflict of beliefs' cannot be seen exclusively under the ethical aspect of a relation between self-understandings which mutually enrich each other.

II

Two contrary (and oversimplified) answers have been given to the following question: Can those who belong to different cultures meet on a common basis of understanding, and where might this universal, all-embracing commonality be found? The self-conscious *universalism* of the Western tradition begins from the unity of a reason which is innate in every human being. It uses the current standards of science or philosophy as the guideline for a binding interpretation of what should be regarded as rational. Against this approach there stands a self-contradictory *relativism*, which assumes that all strong traditions have their own incommensurable criteria of the true and the false, criteria which are internal to them. These two views articulate different conceptions of rationality. While abstract universalism dismisses the insights of the historical sciences of culture, relativism allows itself to be overwhelmed by them. On the one side the various religious truths fall victim to the critique of a unified reason; on the other this universal reason shatters into a kaleidoscope of incompatible truths. Given such assumptions, intercultural understanding would be either unproblematic or meaningless.

More reflective answers to the challenge of historicism can be found in another direction, most obviously in *contextualism*, which is equally sceptical about the assumption of a universal human reason. On this view, unconditional validity claims only appear in local versions, and are so deeply immersed in the context of a specific tradition that the

criteria of their truth and falsehood are inseparably interwoven with a concrete understanding of self and world. Of
course, Alasdair MacIntyre or Richard Rorty would like to
avoid the paradoxical standpoint of the relativist, who must
exempt her own statements from the context-dependency of
all other statements. MacIntyre assumes that one tradition
can indeed show itself to be superior to others; but because
of the incommensurability of their criteria, different traditions cannot communicate seriously with each other or even
learn from each other. Amidst the clash of competing world
pictures, the truth of the superior tradition emerges solely by
virtue of the fact that the inferior side abandon their own
standards of rationality. They seek an escape from their
epistemological crisis through conversion. Rorty begins in
sound hermeneutic style by securing his own context, but
he then holds fast to this in a *one-sided* way. He espouses a
nonchalant ethnocentrism which is based on those standards
which *we* regard as the best. On his view intercultural understanding takes the form of an assimilating inclusion of the
alien within one's own ever-expanding universe.

Philosophical hermeneutics opposes this assimilationist
model with a dialogical model of understanding. Here too
the initial context in which the intepreter finds herself is not
leapt over in favour of the supposed objectivity of understanding. But the dialogical situation in which speaker and
hearer, the interpreting questioner and the answering author
(or her text) find themselves, is characterized by a relational
symmetry. Understanding is only possible between parties
who expect to be able to learn from each other. Through
the exchange of first- and second-person perspectives, which
are reciprocally related to each other, they are able to
effect a *rapprochement* between the divergent horizons of
their linguistic pre-understanding. Thus hermeneutics wrests
the universalistic potential of a linguistically embodied
reason from the conditions of successful communication as
such, and encourages us in the quest for intercultural understanding.

But it is still unclear what goal such a quest should orient-
ate itself towards. Should it aim for a possible substantive

agreement? Or, taking account of the kinds of disagreement which may reasonably be expected, should it have the more modest goal of mutual respect for the sincerely attested power of opposed traditions? The different answers to this question are closely connected with how we understand the process of enlightenment. Depending on how we view the Enlightenment which occurred in Europe in the modern period, we draw the line between faith and knowledge, between the spheres in which we may reasonably expect agreement or disagreement, in different ways. The dividing line concerns the triple relation of philosophy (1) to its own history; (2) to the interconnection of the Old and New Testaments within the Western tradition; and (3) to other world religions in general.

(1) Those who regard the history of philosophy as a continuum, and seek to *level out* the transition from tradition to modernity, will hold fast to the questions and intentions of the great philosophers of the past. They will do this either – like Hegel – in a constructive, or – like Heidegger – in a deconstructive manner. But in any event they will want to recuperate the truth content of the great philosophical tradition in some way. But in this case the affirmatively or negatively preserved claim to comprehensive knowledge will allow no space within philosophy for the distinction between faith and knowledge. Those who *intensify* the break between tradition and modernity will dismiss the knowledge-claims of classical philosophy as extravagant, from the standpoint of a critique of metaphysics. As a result, a greater or lesser proportion of the inherited fund of problems will be transferred to the domain of mere belief. A more or less pedantic scientism, for example, will regard the 'scientific method' as defining the space of possible knowledge. More liberal approaches might also accept questions of justice and of taste into the universe of rationally soluble problems. For Kant there was even a religion within the bounds of reason alone.

(2) With regard to biblical tradition, philosophy has basically adopted one of three positions. It has allowed itself

to be put in the service of religion, in the form of either a positive or a negative theology, or it has at least accepted a co-operative division of labour between natural reason and revelation. Alternatively, in an abstract negation, it has asserted its independence, either polemically or through indifference. Finally, it has claimed cognitive superiority, in the sense that it sought to salvage the truth content of the Judaeo-Christian tradition in its own conceptual terms.

(3) In the face of other religions Western philosophy was very rarely sympathetic or even generous. In this respect Jaspers represents an interesting exception. Certainly, he stresses the gulf between modernity and tradition. But he sets Greek metaphysics alongside the great world religions and assigns it a place within a more comprehensive process of the overcoming of myth, one which is driven forward on both wings. On the other hand, Jaspers describes the constellation of postmetaphysical thinking from the perspective of the faiths which are currently in competition with each other. He even assigns modern philosophy, which he situates between science and theology, to the domain of faith rather than that of knowledge. With these two decisions Jaspers draws an unusual line between faith and knowledge. He recognizes in the self-critical confrontation of modern thought with its own metaphysical beginnings one instance of a more general problem. How can there be rational communication with those faiths which are articulated in strong traditions and in comprehensive doctrines, and which appear to the unbeliever only in the form of ciphers?

III

Jaspers regards the transition to modernity and to postmetaphysical thinking as a profoundly ambivalent process. On the one hand, the Enlightenment frees us from the dogmatism of a faith based on inherited authority. Such faith ties the believer's understanding of herself and of the world to the literal interpretation of a truth-content which can only be communicated in ciphers. Enlightened thought sees through the illusion of this embodiment of transcendence. Like Zwingli, with his critique of Luther's literal notion of transubstantiation, Jaspers aims to take the prohibition of images seriously by treating metaphysical and religious doctrines as so many encodings of fundamental experiences which are inaccessible to conceptual explanation. The philosophical reading of inherited ciphers breaks with the dogmatics of unconditional truth claims: 'I cease to claim that the cipher of the God whom I follow as mine is the God for all.'[5] To this extent enlightenment with respect to metaphysics and religion simply continues that work of disenchantment which metaphysics and religion has once directed against myth. On the other hand, this philosophical translation of symbolic meanings courts the danger that the enciphered truth-contents of the great traditions will be *entirely* forfeited, while the modern sciences reduce the lifeworld to the domain of the objectively knowable and technically controllable: 'The renunciation of the living embodiment of transcendence can result in the ciphers no longer being taken seriously and understood as the language of transcendence, so that they no longer illuminate the space of existence.'[6]

This diagnosis creates a task for philosophy which points beyond the boundaries of scientific knowledge: it must disclose and preserve the truth-content concealed in the semantic potentials of traditions shattered by enlightenment. By contrast with the sciences, philosophy moves in the space of essential – in other words: existential – experiences, a space which is occupied and structured by faith. But, in contrast to tradition, it retrieves these experiences with the argumentative tools of postmetaphysical thinking. In opposition to Kierkegaard, Jaspers's aim is to thematize the experiences which find expression in the Bible, without slipping into the mode of a belief in revelation. He lays claim to a reflective religiosity without certainty of salvation, and treats Kierkegaard as the Young Hegelians treated Hegel. Just as the former strove to retain the dialectical self-movement of Spirit without accepting the notion of absolute Spirit, so

Jaspers would like to complete the transition from the ethical to the religious stage, without arriving at Jesus Christ.

A further implication of the connection to Kierkegaard is that philosophy, which can no longer be either science or theology, must restrict itself to being a 'philosophy of existence'. It must propose the kind of ethics which is possible *after* metaphysics, and which lacks the support of being embedded in the context of a comprehensive interpretation of the world. Fundamental philosophical knowledge establishes the conceptual framework for a possible ethical-existential self-understanding. In Jaspers's own words, it allows for an 'illumination of existence' (*Existenzerhellung*), through which we seek to ascertain who we are and who we want to be. But a clear understanding of one's own existence cannot be achieved without an equally clear understanding of the world. One's own existence cannot be illuminated without a enlightened account of 'transcendence'. This is Jaspers's name for that which always sustains and emcompasses us. This all-embracing reality (*das Umgreifende*) is another expression for the horizon of the linguistically structured life-world, within which we always already find ourselves. We find ourselves within it in three different respects: as self-asserting subjects in the struggle for existence, as an impersonal consciousness in general in objectifying thought, and as communicatively socialized – and thus also individuated – members of an ethical community held together by shared ideas. To the extent that we become aware of the primordial phenomenon of the world which encompasses us – or of transcendence – we gain the freedom for ethical transformation and for becoming a self, for the conscious conduct of our lives as unique individuals.

In contrast to Heidegger, Jaspers gives this positive turn towards authenticity an emphatically intersubjective interpretation. We receive the encouragement and guidance which make us want to be a self only from communication with another self: 'Being a self and being in communication are inseparable.'[7] Jaspers is thinking here of ethical-existential conversation, in which we gain greater clarity concerning our own life-orientation. He does not conceive of this

conversation on the model of clinical discussion with a thera-
pist, one which might have suggested itself to him as a
psychiatrist. Rather, he describes it as a friendly yet polem-
ical engagement with competing life projects. In our encounter with the existence of others we get clearer about the faith
from which our own existence draws its strength. Thus
existential communication takes the form of a struggle of
beliefs. What is disputed is how to read the ciphers of these
beliefs, and how to release their semantic potential through
the right conduct of life. The beliefs embodied in antagonistic forms of life encounter each other in an ambivalence of
attraction and repulsion. What attracts or repels, namely
strong evaluations, occupies the place of the true and the
false: 'To understand each other through ciphers implies a
form of communication in contact with the transcendent.
Here the most intimate tie can be accompanied by the
most remarkable hostility.'[8]

IV

Before I return to the question of what we might learn from
all this for the intercultural understanding needed today, I
must highlight one problematic issue. Jaspers does not regard
his description of the fundamental situation of human beings
as a merely formal theory of the authentic or unspoiled
life, one which clarifies general conditions of any possible
ethical-existential self-understanding. For him, fundamental
philosophical knowledge takes the form of a substantive
ethic, which indicates how one should practise being a self.
It is clear that Jaspers describes the conditions for gaining a
secure sense of self and for being a self from the perspective
of a specific tradition, namely a philosophically appropriated
version of the tradition of the Reformation. He makes no
attempt to disguise this fact when he describes his own
philosophy as 'faith', as an expression – albeit highly reflective – of a specific form of belief. Philosophy experiences the
antagonism of the beliefs which it investigates within itself.

As philosophical faith it can appear only in plural forms, and can no more claim universal validity than the metaphysical or religious doctrines whose truth content it seeks to save. Of course, 'this philosophical faith, which appears in many forms...cannot [become] an authority or a dogma, [it] remains dependent on communication between human beings, who are obliged to talk to each other, but not necessarily to pray with each other.'[9]

But this way of drawing the line between faith and knowledge is problematic in view of the interpretive role which philosophy must *also* take on. For if fundamental philosophical knowledge is distinguished from the comprehensive doctrines of the tradition only by virtue of its undogmatic posture, then it lacks the impartiality which is needed if it is to establish the rational basis on which *contrary* faiths can enter into a fruitful communication with each other. Jaspers does not distinguish clearly enough between the two tasks which he assigns to philosophy, including his own. As the ethical project of a truthfully lived existence it is an advertisement for one form of faith amongst others. But in so far as it analyses the conditions for a successful communication between essentially competing faiths, then its arguments must be directed towards an agreement concerning the rules of the game, in other words they must *point beyond* substantive ethical questions, concerning which there can always be reasonable dissent. The same tension can be found in John Rawls's 'political liberalism'. Rawls draws similar conclusion to Jaspers from the fact of a plurality of world views. Here too philosophy appears in a strange double role. In the form of substantive metaphysical doctrines it raises strong truth claims which cannot, however, be universalized. Such doctrines cannot expect to achieve a rational consensus in their competition with similarly comprehensive religious doctrines. In the role of a theory of justice, philosophy changes sides; but even then it puts forward a form of 'knowledge' which remains dependent on the approval of the various faiths. Connected with the 'thin' conception of justice which political philosophy proposes is simply the hope for an acceptance which would be based on a fortunate convergence of non-public reasons. This conception has to wait to find out whether its proposal is sufficiently neutral to find access to all the competing world views. With his distinction between the strong 'truths' of metaphysical and religious doctrines and the weak 'rationality' of political conceptions of justice, Rawls makes explicit what remains implicit in Jaspers. He highlights the tension between the context-dependent, but existentially relevant truths of philosophical faith on the one hand, and the rationally acceptable results of the analysis of *general* conditions of communication on the other.

In Rawls, the scope of the reason which we share extends to the conditions of a just political life, and not simply, as in Jaspers, to a mutual acknowledgement concerning divergent conceptions of a fulfilled life. Intercultural understanding must be considered from both angles – from the angle of the good, as well as from that of justice.

V

Jaspers seeks to answer the question

> whether all human beings on the globe could eventually find common ground in the universal reason which [in the form of existential communication – J. H.] is projected as the essential form of association with others. Is a maximal shared framework possible, within which the communication of historically heterogeneous faiths ... could occur, without their being abandoned? Could they be transmuted into new forms through a return to their own deepest sources, forms which could give purpose to human life in the context of the presently dawning epoch of world history?[10]

This formulation is not entirely unambiguous. For at first glance Jaspers seems to be expecting that, *after the Enlightenment*, strong traditions will abandon their dogmatic claims to truth and that, instructed by insight into the fundamental situation of human beings, they will transform themselves into versions of philosophical faith.

This intepretation would be tantamout to announcing the death of religions, whose capacity for survival can scarcely be doubted in the current world situation. It is also inconsistent with Jaspers's own reflections. From his standpoint, philosophers and others committed to a set of beliefs encounter each other under premises which do indeed differ, but which do not exclude meaningful communication. The enlightened philosopher sees in the adherents of a metaphysical or religious doctrine simply the members of different communities of interpretation, each of which is united around its own conception of the good life. Conversely, the religious person is convinced that philosophers who describe faith as an *ethical* conception miss the *redemptive* significance and binding character of prophetically disclosed truths, and deprive their own lives of an essential dimension.

When we understand Jaspers in this way, we come up against the problem I have already mentioned. The difficulty is that even philosophical faith remains one party to disputes amongst others. In actual fact, only an impartial fundamental knowledge could foster the desired communication *between* different forms of belief. In this role, fundamental knowledge acquires an entirely different meaning. For then its function is to disclose to religious and metaphysical world views their own inherent reflexivity, exploiting the reflective advance which they experience within themselves under conditions of a pluralism of world views. Philosophy, which has passed through the Enlightenment, and has had to come to terms with its own metaphysical beginnings, eludicates the difference between religion *before* and religion *after* the Enlightenment. It teaches other traditions about that distancing step away from themselves which reason requires them to take as soon as they become aware that they share the same universe of validity-claims with other faiths.

The pluralism of world views means that comprehensive doctrines, whether across the globe or within the same political community, come into conflict concerning the truth of their declarations, the rightness of their commandments, and the credibility of their promises. At the same time, they cannot restrict themselves to the kinds of reasons which can expect general public acknowledgement in modern societies. However, from the standpoint of world views, this form of reflection leads neither to the abandonment of essentialist truth-claims nor to the reinterpretation of truth-claims as context-dependent claims to authenticity. It only makes clear that in the case of controversial existential questions arising from differing world views even the most rationally conducted discursive engagement will not lead to consensus. In the case of these questions of ethical self-understanding, in which the perspective of the first person singular or plural is inscribed, it is reasonable to expect continuing disagreement. As I have mentioned, Jaspers expects the result of successful existential communication to be 'unanimity'. But this concerns only the mutual respect which the participants offer each other, once they have convinced themselves of the authenticity of another form of life whose self-understanding they do not share.

This expectation can also inform attempts at intercultural understanding, to the extent that these aim to foster the mutual esteem of alien cultures and ways of life, despite differences in fundamental value-orientations. However, this form of communication cannot even begin, unless there is a prior consensus concerning important *preconditions* of communication. The relevant parties must renounce the violent imposition of their convictions – an imposition by military, governmental or terroristic means. They must acknowledge each other as partners with equal rights, regardless of their reciprocal *evaluations* of traditions and forms of life. They must also acknowledge each other as participants in a discussion in which, as a matter of principle, each side can learn from the other. In this respect the overcoming of a fundamentalistic self-understanding – of a 'fanaticism which breaks off all communication' – implies not only the reflexive tempering of dogmatic truth-claims, in other words a *cognitive* self-limitation, but also the transition to a different stage of moral consciousness. The boundless 'will to communication' invoked by Jaspers is driven by a moral insight which precedes everything which can be disclosed *within* existential communication. I mean the insight that intercultural understanding can only succeed under conditions of symmetrically conceded freedoms, a reciprocal willingness to view things from the perspective of the other. Only then can a political culture develop which is also sensitive to the need for the institution-alization of appropriate preconditions of communication, in the form of human and constitutional rights.

Of course, Jaspers was alert to the fact that hermeneutical insights have political consequences. He perceives that reason, which tames fundamentalism, is built into the com-municative constitution of our socio-cultural forms of life. Out of the logic of question and answer he unfolds a concep-tion of truth and knowledge which has passed through the filter of the philosophy of language. The objectivity of knowledge is structurally dependent on the intersubjective conditions of its communicability: 'The answers which the world gives to our questions take the form of facts...the questions which the world poses to us take the form of situations, of the unexpected. Only human beings can trans-form mute events into an interplay, by responding as though communication were taking place.'[11] Yet, as a philosopher of existence, Jaspers was so obsessed with ethical self-under-standing, with 'communication in the domain of uncondi-tional truths',[12] that he failed to exploit the normative resources of communicative reason in the domains of mor-ality, law and politics.[13]

Notes

1   K. Jaspers, *Der philosophische Glaube angesichts der Offenbar-ung* (Munich: Piper, 1984), p. 7.
2   Ibid., p. 317.
3   K. Jaspers, *The Great Philosophers*, tr. Ralph Manheim (Lon-don: Rupert Hart-Davis, 1962).
4   K. Jaspers, *Schelling* (Munich: Piper, 1955).
5   *Der philosophische Glaube*, p. 428.
6   Ibid., p. 438.
7   K. Jaspers, *Von der Wahrheit* (1947) (Munich: Piper, 1991), p. 546.
8   *Der philosophische Glaube*, p. 205.

9   Ibid., p. 110.
10 Ibid., p. 148.
11 *Von der Wahrheit*, p. 643.
12 Ibid., p. 975.
13 H. Fahrenbach, 'Kommunikative Vernunft – ein zentraler Bezugspunkt zwischen Karl Jaspers und Jürgen Habermas', in K. Salamun, ed., *Karl Jaspers* (Munich: Piper, 1991), pp. 189–216.

3

Between Traditions

A Laudatio *for Georg Henrik von Wright*

I am delighted to have received this invitation from the University of Leipzig. For it honours me with the opportunity to offer my personal thanks to Georg Henrik von Wright for what I have learned from him over many decades. But how is one to praise someone who has already received so much praise, honour someone who has so often received honours, appreciate a body of work which has been appreciated so many times? On the occasion of this academic celebration it is certainly appropriate to recall the outstanding achievements of Georg Henrik von Wright, which have decisively influenced the direction of both Continental and Anglo-Saxon philosophy in the second half of this century. But I would also like to investigate the 'motivational background' without which, according to von Wright's own theory, actions cannot be properly understood. For after all, philosophizing – too – is a form of practice.

Innovative impulses were already at work in the young scholar's dissertation, and in the treatises on induction and probability which emerged from it. Decades later, well-known philosophers of science were to engage with this first text, in the volume of the celebrated 'Library of Living Philosophers' devoted to the mature work of the Finnish philosopher, who

---

Lecture given on 21 May 1996 at the University of Leipzig.

was now world-famous. As early as 1951 a pioneering essay on deontic logic appeared in *Mind*, an essay which attracted international attention to this 35-year-old disciple of Wittgenstein. In a splendid example of what Peirce called inductive imagination, von Wright describes the sudden insight which he had as he was walking by the river in Cambridge, and which inspired his influential investigation. He suddenly realized that the deontic modalities of the required, the permitted and the forbidden behave in a logically similar way to the modalizations of the actual, of truth and of knowledge.

His two further steps, first from the logical investigation of normative expressions to the logic of preferences, and then from the theory of values to the theory of action, can be seen in retrospect as a continuous development. But the image of a quantum leap is more appropriate. For the extension of logical analysis to value-orientations and agents' intentions was not due, like that first step, to an expansion of logic itself, but to a shift of perspective which brought entirely new facts and relations into view. The tools of logic served here for the clarification of intuitions which point beyond the domain of propositions. This is true, for example, of the almost Kantian idea that the concept of causality is connected with the possibility of intervening in a rule-governed process, and to this extent is dependent on concepts of human intervention and of the capacity for action. It is also true of the view that actions are internally connected with the reasons for which the actor carries them out. In *Explanation and Understanding*, published in 1971, von Wright connects these two thoughts to produce a dualistic conception of the sciences. This conception emphasized the autonomy and independence of the hermeneutic procedures of the cultural and social sciences, by contrast with the metholodological ideal of the natural sciences, and thereby gave a new impetus to the old controversy between explanation and understanding.

As the topic of the lecture which he has announced for the present occasion, 'The Place of Psychology in the Sciences', suggests, von Wright's interest in the basic concepts and explanatory strategies of the human sciences has not diminished. It is only the emphasis which has shifted. The old theme of the relation of mind and body has acquired new relevance in the face of the challenge of the cognitive sciences. At this point of intersection between disciplines, the humanistic motive which, from the very beginning, has guided his researches as a logician becomes clear. His desire is to do justice to the undeniable phenomenon of human freedom, as the capacity to act rationally. As a logician, von Wright is inspired by the pathos of scientific clarity. He has always submitted his work to strict analytical criteria and engaged in philosophy as a science. But at the same time, he has no wish to make philosophy *dissolve* into science. He shares Wittgenstein's feeling that 'even when all scientific questions have been answered, the problems of our life have not been touched on at all'. Admittedly, he does not pursue the same path as Wittgenstein, or indeed Heidegger. He does not seek to break out of academic philosophy. He makes use of its tools to take an unpretentious step beyond the limits of an academicized philosophy which is now *only* preoccupied with its own internal problems.

As a humanist, von Wright has no wish to absolve philosophy of a duty to help the lifeworld achieve a secure sense of itself through self-criticism. Philosophy should investigate problems which are posed for all of us by life itself, whether we are philosophers or not. Here I am thinking not just of von Wright's commitments as a citizen and an intellectual, as someone who has participated in public discussion of contentious issues. It is true that the voice which he has raised in the public political arena has been heard beyond the boundaries of Scandinavia. But today I am interested in something different, namely the contribution which von Wright has made to orientating knowledge as a postmetaphysical philosopher. Referring to his non-philosophical writing, he once remarked:

> I think that one motive behind my essay-writing activities was a sense of the discrepancy between the narrowly restricted relevance and scope of my professional work and the drive which I always felt to make philosophy relevant to my life and my understanding of the world. Perhaps one reason why I gradually abandoned these activities was

that this rift in my philosophical personality ... has begun to heal.

This existential motive endows even his acute contributions to highly specialized academic debates with a meaning which points beyond the details. More specifically, out of the complex interconnection of these elements there emerges a suggestive perspective on contemporary possibilities for the self-conscious conduct of life. Von Wright's philosophical labours are all directed towards the central issue of an anthropology of the self-determining life. Here both things come together: the results of an argument pursued over decades, but also the experiences of a life history which has been reflected upon. These are the experiences not just of an intellectually remarkable individual, but also of a genuinely moral person, someone of real independence in judgement and action, with the delightful charm of a cultured European of the old school, and a typically Scandinavian civility.

From the beginning von Wright found himself torn between two traditions. Philosophically, he passed through the school of logical empiricism, which originated in Vienna, but expanded and established itself in America and Scandinavia. In his personal orientation he was formed far more by a conservative – one might say Burckhardtian – cultural outlook. He stood between traditions – one of which regarded itself as modernistic, as part of an expanding progressive movement, while the other took up a quietistic or even defensive attitude towards the impulses of the new age. Von Wright has been inspired by both traditions. But in the course of his development he has also gained a certain distance from them. Today he no longer has any difficulty in combining Kant with Musil, and Wittgenstein with Marx.

This background helps to explain his untypical relation to Wittgenstein, his honoured teacher. On the one hand, von Wright senses the affinities of outlook. He is confident that he is better able to understand the complexities of this extraordinary mind than Wittgenstein's own mesmerized followers. Significantly, of the three literary executors, it was he who published the 'Vermischte Bemerkungen' in 1977, giving us a first glimpse of Wittgenstein's cultural pessimism, his out-and-out Spenglerian diagnosis of the times. The critical attitude towards science and the religious posture, the concealed metaphysical impulses, which these notes reveal, throw an ironic light on the influence of both the earlier and the later Wittgenstein – on the misunderstanding of the *Tractatus* in the Vienna Circle of the 1920s, but also on the lack of sympathy for the speculative ambitions of the *Philosophical Investigations* which was typical of their reception by enthusiastic British and American adherents after the Second World War. Even during his time in Cambridge von Wright must have sensed the dissonances between the horizon of expectations of the Anglo-Saxon philosophical world, and the aspirations of a genius who grew up in turn-of-the-century Vienna.

On the other hand, despite everything which he learned from him, Von Wright did not become one of Wittgenstein's pupils. He did not allow the latter's inimitable style of thought to lure him away from his analytically perspicuous mode of argumentation. Nor did he allow his view of the times to be infected by Wittgenstein's emotional responses, derived as they were from a very German tradition of *Kulturkritik*. Von Wright himself has described the liberating effect which the forward-looking pragmatism of American scientific culture had on him, as a European intellectual with a very different outlook. This influence appears in the final sentence of his book on Wittgenstein: 'His [Wittgenstein's] conception of philosophy is closely bound up with a perspective on contemporary civilization – this much must be agreed. But it is another question whether this perspective has to be that of Spengler.'

Von Wright regards his own philosophical work as a rational reconstruction of conceptual intuitions, one which can be guided neither by the actual nor solely by the correct use of linguistic expressions. It proceeds simultaneously in a constructive and a disclosing manner. The initially puzzling appearance of the deep grammatical structure of a field of fundamental concepts can be dissolved through interpolation, through the 'filling out of blank spaces'. The reconstructive work gets its driving impulse from puzzles which only the philosophically trained eye can bring to light. A good example is the problem with which the brilliant treatise on 'Is and Ought' dating from 1985 begins: how can we justify the expansion of traditional logic beyond the frame of the true and the false?

Von Wright has in fact remained true to his logical empiricist beginnings in one respect: in ethical questions he defends a non-cognitive position. Normative statements can be neither true nor false. They state what should be done, whereas the point of statements which are descriptive or capable of truth is to represent what is the case. On these assumptions, the mere fact of deontic logic throws up a disturbing question. On the one hand, such a logic analyses relations between prescriptive sentences and thus appears to submit to its laws a body of statements which are incapable of truth. On the other hand, logical relations such as consequence and contradiction have the clear status of truth-preserving or truth-destroying relations between statements. Consequently it seems that, in contradiction to the non-cognitivist position, the capacity for truth of these statements has to be presupposed. This paradox provides the starting point for a reconstruction of the fundamental concepts of a practice regulated by norms.

A dissolution of the paradox becomes possible when one distinguishes between the social fact of the existence of norms expressing the will of a norm-positing authority, on the one hand, and prescriptive sentences which refer to the content of norms on the other. It then becomes clear why norms which conflict with each other can co-exist, whereas the corresponding normative statements contradict each other. An irrationally acting law-giver can very easily issue norms which have contradictory content, whereas it is logically impossible for the addressees to carry out his commands simultaneously. After this preparatory move von Wright can present deontic logic as a means of testing the consistency of legislation. It investigates logical relations in the deontically perfect world of completely rational legislation. Thus deontic logic can be considered as 'a genuine expansion of the frame of logic beyond the domain of the true and the false towards that of rationality', namely the rationality of the practice of norm-positing and legislation in general.

I have introduced this example, which is meant to show the meaning which Carnap's expression 'rational reconstruction' takes on in von Wright's work, with a further intention. For I am not convinced that the 'theory of willing', according to which norms can be seen as the expressions of the will of a power-holder, really captures our intuitions. Normative expectations are distinguished from mere expressions of will by their *obligatory* character, which derives from the validity-claims of the underlying norms themselves. For members of a community who normatively regulate their common life, norms mean something different than they do for the sociological observer: they are not just social facts, but expectations of behaviour, whose binding normative character displays a certain affinity with the rationally motivating force of true statements. From the perspective of participants, we agree with norms in a way which is not identical with, but is *similar* to the way we agree with assertoric sentences we regard as true. Should this intuition turn out to be not entirely misleading, then we would perhaps have to reconsider the narrowness of a semantic notion of truth, which is the basis for the thesis that normative statements can neither be valid nor invalid.

A *laudatio* is not the place for a discussion of contentious issues. I have alluded to my reservations only to lure us onto a track which – in my view – von Wright himself has laid down. The longer I immerse myself in his work of recent decades, the more I feel strengthened in the suspicion that the voluntaristic conception of norms and a non-cognitive understanding of morality and law are problematic. They seem increasingly incompatible with the concept of human freedom, and the conception of a life fit for human beings, which emerge ever more clearly from his arguments. This suspicion prompts me to conclude with three series of comments. First, I would like to recall the observation with which Georg Meggle begins his lucid and instructive engage-

ment with von Wright: he claims that, in his analyses of
understanding and explanation, von Wright has moved ever
closer to Wittgenstein's conception of rule-guided action.
The second remark relates to the consequences which this
conception of following a norm has for the concept of freedom. This brings me, finally, to the question of whether von
Wright, in the course of his long and productive intellectual
development, which leads from Vienna, via Cambridge, to
Helsinki, has arrived at a complex concept of understanding
which explodes the limits of Aristotelian 'phronesis'
and incorporates elements of Kant's concept of practical
reason.

(1) In order to understand a given action, we have to
know the reasons for which the actor carried it out. In this
context von Wright has always distinguished internal from
external reasons, in other words value preferences and purposes from signals and demands. But only gradually has one
kind of external reason especially attracted his attention:
orders, questions, promises, regulations, rules of all kinds.
For such norms can be accommodated by the intentionalistic
model of action only as long as the sanctions which may be in
place to back them up provide the decisive reason for actors
to behave in accordance with them. In general, however, the
background of social interaction consists of more or less
habitual norms which we follow because we have implicitly
recognized them, or because we see no reason to deviate
from them. The norm itself is reason enough; it would be
rather artificial to ascribe yet a *further* intention to actors in
such cases, for example the intention of 'not wanting to
deviate from what it usual' (Meggle). The intention of following a given norm *is* the intention to behave correctly;
since only the norm tells us what 'right behaviour' is. For
this reason von Wright draws a clear distinction between the
case of preference-guided action (in Max Weber's sense of
the appropriate choice of means to achieve a goal) and that of
conventional or rule-guided action (to which he also assimilates speech acts – which amounts to an implicit rejection of
intentionalist theories of meaning). In this way he does justice to the distinction between legality and morality, or more

generally, that between action guided by consequences, which merely happens to conform to an existing norm, and the direct following of an implicitly recognized or expressly accepted rule.

(2) What does this distinction imply for the concept of freedom? Von Wright has devoted what I regard as his finest essay to this topic. Here what is primarily at issue is that freedom of choice which Kant understood as the capacity of an actor to *commit herself* to a maxim of action. Von Wright starts from the intuition that we act freely precisely when we could have behaved differently in a specific situation: 'The fact that an actor acted for a particular reason normally means that something was a reason for this actor to do something, and that he *set about* doing this thing *for that reason*. When one says this, one suggests that he could in fact have acted otherwise.' On this view, the freedom of an actor essentially consists in the capacity to establish such a connection between a reason and an action, so that he acts *for this reason*. It is only this connection which *generates* actions, and an actor under-stands himself *as* an agent when he attributes this act of generation to himself. To 'set about' acting for a specific reason means, precisely, deciding to carry out this action. (This is why we understand another's action when we can make sense of her self-understanding or, in the case of self-deception, agree with her retrospectively on a better self-understanding.)

Naturally, there are external and internal limitations of freedom – constraining circumstances or psychological com-pulsions which, in a specific situation, prevent us from carry-ing out an action which we would normally have performed, because we currently have a sufficient reason to do so, and in general also have the capacity. Of course, such limitations do not always have the character of physical impediments or psychic inhibitions, which our intentions *shatter* against. Often they are prescriptive limits, as in the case of action guided by norms. An interesting case can occur here, one in which we do not experience moral, or legal, or purely habitual rules as limitations of our freedom.

For norms cannot stand opposed to our intentions when these intentions have a fortiori already been formed by them. The really significant case is that of moral duties: 'Internal normative limitations on the freedom of an actor are prohibitions which the actor *recognizes* as duties which he must fulfil. They can also be called self-imposed limitations.' There then follows the reflective remark: 'Some have also believed that only actions which are in conformity with self-imposed duties are "really free".' Von Wright sees how the distinction between preference-guided and norm-guided actions can be used, in order to distinguish, as does Kant, between autonomy and freedom of choice.

(3) But can an action performed out of moral duty be called 'free' when such duties derive from the internalization of existing social norms? We could only speak of freedom in cases where the agent makes the obligatory norm on which her action is based her own, and does so 'of her own accord', or with 'will and consciousness'. She must have chosen these norms for good reasons. The act of self-legislation should not be interpreted voluntaristically. Von Wright continues the hypothetical reflection just mentioned as follows: 'If one wished to argue that true freedom consists in action guided by norms, then one would have to argue that the reasons which are provided by norms of a particular kind, whether they be the laws of the state or those of our moral consciousness, are the best reasons for which we can act.'

But how does one decide which reasons are the best? Reasons force themselves upon us; it does not lie within the freedom of the agent himself 'to have the reasons which he actually has'. Many reasons spring from our needs and preferences, others from our education or traditions. Von Wright considers the idea that an actor can perhaps decide all the more freely, the *more* reasons he has at his disposal. He thereby suggests a connection between freedom and understanding, between emancipation and the *expansion* of our horizon of understanding, which is illuminating from a humanistic point of view. This fits in with another idea which has been developed within the theory of values. Norm-guided action is always the action of members of a society integrated by means of values. And here a perspective opens from which we can *evaluate* the reasons for the choice of norms. This is because, for members of such a society, those reasons are best which can count on general agreement. And these reasons will select those norms which are in the equal interest of everyone. It is in this Kantian sense that I like to interpret the conclusion which von Wright draws from considerations which are rather more Aristotelian than Kantian in tone: 'Symmetry and universalizability seem to be two indicators which lead us to regard it as rational to have certain attitudes towards our fellow human beings.' With this interpretation I have tried in my own way to respond to the implicit demand which every significant philosopher places on his readers: to think further with the author against the author himself.

4

Tracing the Other of History in History

Gershom Scholem's Sabbatai Ṣevi

Sixteen years after the publication of the English original, a German translation of Gershom Scholem's *The Main Currents of Jewish Mysticism* appeared in 1957. Those who regarded this book, when it came out in Germany, as the masterwork of a great scholar of the Kabbalah were soon obliged to revise their views. For in the same year Scholem published a large-scale biography of Sabbatai Ṣevi, who converted to Islam in 1666, the *kairos* of the heretical movement which he had launched. The work did not appear in English until 1973, in an expanded version authorized by Scholem. And almost two more decades were to elapse before the Jüdische Verlag published the long-planned German edition of this version. The book is 1093 pages in length; but this number would not satisfy Scholem's taste for kabbalistic number games. Once, while I was visiting him in Jerusalem, he presented me with an English copy of *Sabbatai Ṣevi*, and opened the last page with a meaningful look: it bore the round figure 1000. Perhaps he was thinking of the utopian features of those millenarian movements which – at the end of *our* millennium – are regarded with a good deal of scepticism. Of course, Scholem knew that page numbers are accidental. And yet, with his mischievous gesture, he wanted to leave open the question of whether this was *merely* chance.

———
Article published in *Babylon*, nos 10–11, 1992.

The intentional ambiguity of this gesture is typical of the scholar's work as a whole. As a historian, he musters in his arsenal all the techniques of critical literary scholarship in order to search for a truth which is distorted, rather than disclosed, by the historical tradition. This applies not only to the truth about the Sabbatianic movement. In general, Scholem regarded philological studies of the history of the Kabbalah as an ironic line of business: 'Does something of the inner law of what is fundamentally at issue remain visible to the philologist, or does what is essential disappear in this projection of the historical? The uncertainty of the answer to this question belongs to the nature of philosophical questioning as such; and so the hope which sustains this work is tinged with a certain irony.'[1]

What hope is in question here? The reports of the mystics must have filled Scholem with the kind of expectation which, in earlier generations, was aroused by the words of the prophets. Scholem believed in the gift of mystical illumination. Admittedly, as he once told me, he had encountered such a capacity for inspiration only once in his life – in the person of his friend Walter Benjamin. In a dedication dating from 1941, Scholem characterized the genius of his friend by evoking 'the depth of the metaphysician, the penetration of the critic, and the knowledge of the scholar' – mystical gifts he did not mention. But his lifelong fixation with his friend, the passionate determination with which, right till the very end, he hunted down the scattered traces of the manuscript of the 'Arcades Project', a manuscript which was thought to be lost, suggest that Scholem saw Benjamin as a spirit haunted by illuminations.

But whatever is disclosed to the sight of the inward eye, the mystical vision, evades the word, the medium of tradition. The nature of mystical truth is paradoxical: 'It can be known, but not handed down, and the remains of it which can be handed down no longer contain it.'[2] Scholem searches history for the other of history. The unease which this paradox arouses is at the same time the driving force behind his work as a historian.

This unease also explains his interest in those heretical movements which seek through a praxis of intentional law-

breaking to overcome evil once and for all and to accelerate
the advent of the messianic age. Benjamin discovered antino-
mianism in an entirely different sphere – in contemporary
surrealism, which aimed to release ambivalent feelings
and renew primeval shocks through a calculated attack
on ossified forms of perception. In these aesthetic experi-
ments Scholem could see no more than a feeble imitation
of those antinomian actions which had produced an incom-
parably greater force of renewal. Scholem, the bourgeois
scholar, certainly did not identify with religious extremism.
He reveals unsparingly the pathological traits and charla-
tanry of the ambivalent figure of Sabbatai Ṣevi. But he
also emphasizes the innovative power of heretical movements. In terms of historically accessible documentation,
they offer the most significant proof of the reality of a knowledge which, in its non-verbalizable core, eludes the historical
tradition.

Sabbatianism is of course only the penultimate link in
the chain of the Kabbalah's history, which Scholem has
brought to light from obscure sources and corrupted manu-
scripts.

(1) He deals first of all with the doctrines of Isaak
Luria, who founded a widely influential school in the middle
of the sixteenth century, in Safed in Palestine. Lurian
mysticism breaks in one primary respect with the dominant
conceptions of the kabbalistic doctrine of the high Middle
Ages, the Zohar. The neo-Platonic concepts of the Zohar
could only define the evil and the untrue, and in general
negative phenomena such as the harmful, the diseased
and the hostile, in *privative* terms – as the obscuring or
weakening of the Ideas, as matter sullying ideal being, so to
speak. The negative lacked the spur of wilfulness, the character of the resistant, even the productive. For this reason,
the problem of theodicy was defused right from the beginning. The question of how evil is possible at all in a world
created by God can only be given a coherent formulation
when we take the negative seriously in its distinctive positivity, and lead it back to its origin in the divine life-process
itself.

This is what Luria's original idea of the *tsim-tsum* achieves. God, who in the beginning was everything, withdraws into Himself, implodes as it were, in order to make room for His creatures. Luria's image of the contraction or withdrawal into oneself is intended to explain the void out of which God then created heaven and earth. Through this initial contraction there arises (as Jakob Böhme will put it, in a curious convergence with Lurianic mysticism) a nature in God, a knot of wilfulness and egoity. The polar tension between this dark ground in God and His radiating love already determines the ideal process of creation, which occurs in God's body and thought. This culminates in the figure of the first Adam, Adam Kadmon. Or, more precisely, it would have so culminated, had a catastrophe not intervened. The vessels, which can no longer contain the sparks of divine light, break apart. As a result of this disruptive event, the rest of the process of creation acquires a new meaning: the lights which have been poured away and dispersed must be raised up again to their legitimate place of origin. The resurrection or restitution of the original order – the *tikkun* – would finally have reached its goal with the creation of the second, the earthly Adam, if the catastrophe had not repeated itself through the Fall. This time the process of creation slips out of the hands of God, so to speak. Now, for the first time, the creation emerges from the inner depths of God and continues in the external history of the world.

(2)   The second link in the historical chain of reception of the Kabbalah is the echo which Lurianic mysticism finds amongst the Jewish people – in the century of the great emigrations after the Reconquista and the expulsion of the Jews from Spain. This event was shattering for the whole of Jewry. It lends a new relevance to the primordial biblical experience of exile. In the light of Lurianic mysticism the meaning of this exile for the history of salvation acquires a new interpretation. For it is seen as a repetition of the exile into which God had entered within Himself, prior to all creation. Luria himself presents the original contraction as a banishment which God must impose on Himself in order to

set the process of creation in motion. But now this fraught drama of the becoming of God is transformed into a model of earthly history which promises salvation. For, since the Fall, part of the responsibility for the success of the resurrection of the fallen world has passed over to human beings themselves: 'The historical process and its innermost soul, the religious act of the Jew, prepare the way for the final restitution of all the scattered and exiled lights and sparks ... Every act of man is related to this final task which God has set for His creatures ... The redemption of Israel concludes the redemption of all things.'[3]

For Luria the appearance of the Messiah simply set the seal on the completion of a process of restoration sustained by the believers themselves. In the Jewish communities, which had been marked by the experience of exile and were threatened by further pogroms, the emphasis shifted. Rather than the power of prayer, it is the expectation of the Messiah which now moves into the foreground. An interest in the role and person of the Messiah which is alien to classic Lurianism develops.

(3)   This is why the decisive link in the chain is provided by the doctrine of Nathan of Gaza. Even before his important meeting with Sabbatai Ṣevi, Nathan had visions which led him to interpret the role of the Messiah in a new way. The soul of the Messiah, which had already plunged into the abyss with the 'breaking of the vessels' is held captive by the forces of evil. It is the holy serpent, who is encircled by the serpents of evil. The existence of the Messiah thus becomes profoundly ambivalent. In the last act of the world-historical drama of salvation the dialectic of intensifying darkness which had already occurred twice, in the breaking of the vessels, and in Adam's Fall, repeats itself for the third time. For the Messiah who has plunged into the abyss can finally subdue the ultimate and most obstinate forces of evil only with their own means. Nathan describes this struggle in the form of a commentary on the apocalypse: the Messiah will do astonishing and terrible things, and he will give himself up to martyrdom, in order to fulfil the will of his Creator.

In 1941 Scholem wrote in *Major Trends*:

> It is not my purpose here to present the swift rise and the
> sudden collapse of the Sabbatian movement in 1665 and
> 1666, from Sabbatai Ṣevi's proclamation of his Messianic
> mission to his renunciation of Judaism and adoption of
> Islam when he was led before the Turkish Sultan. I am not
> primarily concerned with the biography of the Messiah and
> his prophet, Nathan of Gaza, nor with the details of the
> tremendous religious mass movement which spread like
> wild-fire through the entire Diaspora – already prepared, as
> it were, for such an event by the new Kabbalism. Suffice it to
> say that very large numbers of people were swept on a tide of
> emotion and underwent the most extravagant forms of
> penance ... But hand in hand with penitence there also
> went boundless joy and enthusiasm, for at last there seemed
> to be visible proof that the sufferings of 1600 years had not
> been in vain. Before redemption had actually come it was felt
> by many to have become a reality. An emotional upheaval of
> immense force took place among the mass of the people.[4]

It is precisely this programme which Scholem then carries
through with an immense effort of historical and philological
erudition. The fact that, out of eight chapters in the book, he
devotes less than one to Nathan of Gaza should not
be allowed to deceive us as to who played the chief role.
Nathan is the director of the play in which Sabbatai Ṣevi is a
marionette.

Sabbatai requests a meeting with Nathan in the spring of
1665, in the first instance to seek peace for his soul. He
comes to him as a patient to a psychiatrist. But it is Nathan
who convinces him in the course of weeks of conversation
that he is called to be the Messiah. And it is only the uncon-
tested authority of the learned Nathan of Gaza which can
convince even the oldest friends and followers of Sabbatai
Ṣevi of his identity as the Messiah:

> Nathan's character was very different from that of Sabbatai
> Ṣevi. We shall look in vain for any of the prophet's outstand-
> ing qualities in the Messiah: tireless activity, unwavering

perseverance without manic-depressive ups and downs, originality of theological thought and considerable literary ability. Sabbatai's fumbling attempts in theology are pale shadows compared to the systematic audacity which made Nathan the first great theologian of heretical kabbalism. With all the charm, dignity and attractiveness of the 'man of sorrows...smitten of God and afflicted', Sabbatai lacked strength of character...Even in his moments of manic exaltation he did not really 'act', and the flurry of provocative gestures spent itself without producing permanent effects. At the height of the movement he remained passive, and his activity exhausted itself in increasingly bizarre and 'strange' acts. The two men complemented each other in a remarkable fashion, and without that combination the Sabbatian movement would never have developed. Sabbatai was a poor leader. Devoid of will power and without a programme of action, he was a victim of his illness and his illusions.[5]

(4)   But if this is Scholem's view of the relation between these two principal figures, why was all his ambition invested in a biography of Sabbatai Ṣevi? Why did he commit himself, with a positivistic fervour worthy of the most prominent scholars of the German Historical School, to the detective work of unearthing the most trivial details of the life of this shady Messiah? And why did he then spend more than 1000 pages presenting them to us in the form of a brilliant historical novel drawing on original sources? In order to answer this question we must turn our attention to the last link in the chain – the reversal of heretical messianism into what Scholem terms 'religious nihilism'.

Scholem investigates this phenomenon using the example of the populist figure Jakob Frank, who appeared in Galicia as the reincarnation of Sabbatai Ṣevi, and in 1759 converted to Catholicism. Jakob Frank, too, pursued the path into the abyss as the subversive path to salvation: 'Abandon all laws and prescriptions, all virtues, modesty and chastity. Abandon holiness itself. Climb down into yourself as into a grave.'[6] Now it is not merely the bizarre actions of the Messiah which the antinomian doctrine of the holiness of sin explains.

Rather, this doctrine is set up as the law of the law-violating praxis of the community as a whole.

What fascinates Scholem about this is the dialectical reversal of Messianism into enlightenment; for the utopian energies released by heretical messianism are directed by the French Revolution towards political goals in the here and now. The Frankist Moses Dobrushka follows this path in an exemplary way. He became a Catholic and, under the name of Thomas von Schönfeld, he became a spokesman for the Enlightenment policies of the Emperor Joseph, founded an order of Free Masons, and after the outbreak of the French Revolution, became a Jacobin in Strasbourg: 'In April 1794, aged forty, he mounted the scaffold with Danton – under the name Junius Frey.'[7] This reversal of religion into enlightenment illuminates the interesting connection between the history of the influence of the Kabbalah and Scholem's self-understanding as a scholar of the Kabbalah. Scholem is a historian who cannot step back behind the threshold of the historical Enlightenment, and yet wants no accommodation with the historicist 'smokescreen, which – in the form of the history of mystical traditions – conceals the space of the very thing itself'. For Scholem enlightenment is our fate, but this does not mean it should have the last word. He always regarded Marx and Freud as the real heretics; he is convinced that even the religious impulses of the last Sabbatians have not dissolved entirely into a political utopia. At the same time, we are all sons and daughters of the French Revolution. Scholem considered the reversal of religion into enlightenment as inevitable as it was unsatisfactory. And his own historical and philological research into the Kabbalah remained caught in this dichotomy.

Scholem had no other recourse than to incorporate the antinomian motive into his own practice; he buried himself in positivism, in order to penetrate through the smokescreen of historical facts from within. By turning outwards, in a resolutely scientist manner, towards the critical disclosure of the historical material, he sought to get nearer to a truth which transcends all history, since it is only revealed to the inner eye. I regard his obsessively detailed work on the biography of Sabbatai Ṣevi, a book which by all the standards of academic art is truly amazing, as being *also* a spiritual exercise – an exercise by means of which Scholem sought at least to *circle ever closer* to the visions of Nathan of Gaza. Only once, in his 'Ten unhistorical statements concerning the Kabbalah', did Scholem lift the visor of the scientific scholar, and reveal himself as a negative theologian. The third section deals with the mediated nature of the know-ledge passed down to us through tradition and interpretation, knowledge which is repeatedly thwarted by the objectless-ness of the highest knowing, since such knowing belongs to the domain of mystical inspiration. Scholem's train of reflec-tion ends with a statement which could almost be regarded as comforting: ' "Who" is the last word of all theory, and it is quite astonishing that theory can go so far as to escape from the "What" to which its beginnings remain bound.'[8]

Notes

1   G. Scholem, 'Zehn unhistorische Sätze über Kabbala', in *Judaica* 3 (Frankfurt am Main: Suhrkamp, 1973), p. 264.
2   Ibid., p. 264.
3   G. Scholem, *Major Trends in Jewish Mysticism* (New York: Schocken Books, 1961), p. 274.
4   Ibid., p. 288.
5   G. Scholem, *Sabbatai Ṣevi. The Mystical Messiah 1626–1676* (London: Routledge and Kegan Paul, 1973), pp. 207–8.
6   G. Scholem, 'Die Metamorphose des häretischen Messianis-mus', in *Judaica* 3, p. 208.
7   Ibid., p. 212.
8   *Judaica* 3, p. 266.

5

A Master Builder with Hermeneutic Tact

The Path of the Philosopher Karl-Otto Apel

Karl-Otto Apel has been teaching with great success in our Department for nearly two decades. Now he is exchanging the status of professor for that of professor emeritus. In the West, Apel must be counted as one of the four or five best-known German philosophers. Any department, in bidding a formal farewell to such a colleague, necessarily honours itself. That is the superficial meaning of this ceremony. But we also intend it to be a philosophical exercise. For this farewell, dear Karl-Otto, has a dialectical meaning; its aim is to secure your continued presence. Henceforth, however, we will be dependent on your good will for your teaching activity. And we want to win this by convincing you, not by persuading you. This is why the Dean has entrusted me, the oldest remaining member of the Department, with the delicate task of showing you that we are fully aware of the stature of your philosophical work, that we *know* what the presence of your thought and of your person means. If you will allow me to exploit the prerogatives of age, I would like to begin with a few personal reminiscences.

This speech was given on 15 May 1990, on the occasion of the retirement of my friend Karl-Otto Apel.

I

When I arrived in Bonn from Zurich in the winter semester of 1950/51 to continue my studies with Rothacker, I encountered, in Philosophical Seminar A, the traditional world of the German university. It is a world which has now sunk without trace. There were two full professors, an assistant, a handful of students, and even fewer doctoral candidates. The latter had been given their own room, behind the room of the director. But the director's room was occupied neither by Rothacker, nor Oskar Becker, nor even by Wilhelm Perpeet, who was the assistant at that time. Rather, it was occupied by a figure whose residence there turned out to be far from accidental, since his presence marked the spirit of the Seminar almost more than that of any other member. This became clear to me on the first Wednesday morning, which was the first meeting of the philosophy class. I was confronted with a typical picture: Rothacker, who was a chain-smoker, broached a theme and then leant back with his cigarettes. He handed over responsibility for the flow of the discussion to the forceful guidance of a younger colleague, whose headlong engagement seemed half to discomfit him, and half to fill him with pride and admiration. Meanwhile we students, feeling slightly dizzy, struggled to keep up with the audacious mind which could construct such amazing synthetic connections. We barely noticed the sporadic efforts of Perpeet to exercise some pedagogical caution, as he struggled to put a brake on the discussion.

Apel belonged to that generation who could draw on experiences of the War, and who were determined, with an almost violent energy, to make good their lost opportunities for learning. Even at the beginning of the 1950s, we younger ones could still sense the ambivalence of those who had returned from the War. Their recent experience of extreme situations gave them a certain sense of superiority, and yet, being older, and having missed out on years of study, they also felt at a disadvantage. At that time, in a climate shaped by Sartre's philosophy of existence, Heidegger's existential ontology had become almost a form of life for Apel. But despite a certain affinity with the lieutenants who returned from the First World War, Apel was never tempted to follow the Young Conservatives of an earlier age on their elitist path towards a heroic nihilism. Apel found philosophical discussion all-consuming; everything about him, down to his vivid gestures, embodied what was then called 'committed thinking'. But his intellectual passion was nourished by moral impulses which bore no trace of ambivalence. He was one of those who refused to allow the suggestive slogans of situationist ethics to hold them back from an unconstrained reckoning with the moral catastrophe of the 1940s. It was he who gave me a copy of *Introduction to Metaphysics*, hot from the press, and pointed out to me the sentence concerning the 'inner truth and greatness of the movement' which was reproduced without commentary. This we had not expected, being far removed from the quarrels of Freiburg. Even without a seminar of his own, Apel became philosophical mentor to a small group of students during those years. What bound us to him then is what has fascinated many generations of students since: in a way which was neither seductive nor mesmerizing, the fundamental concerns of philosophy itself were embodied in his person.

The academic world to which we were introduced was that of Dilthey and the German Historical School, and of South-West German Neo-Kantianism. Our daily fare was the problems of the interpretive *Geisteswissenschaften* and the comparative science of culture, and of a philosophy of language which led back to Humboldt. Rothacker himself did not experience the epistemological problem of historicism in all its acuteness. For he combined the perspectivism of an all-embracing *Verstehen* with anthropological interests, and – fortunately – encouraged us to take seriously the theoretical contributions of the specialized sciences, of cultural anthropology, of research into animal behaviour, above all of psychology (which he still taught). But apart from the respectable, indeed somewhat tedious moralism of figures such as Theodor Litt, from whom Apel borrowed the notion of a series of reflexive stages in the development of mind, a certain liberal openness prevailed. The life history of our philosophy teachers had been marked by a political rupture; a vital nerve had been struck. They were not in the business of teaching us how to pose radical questions, and then answer them in a systematic way.

Apel rebelled against this milieu with a deep, yet totally unpretentious moral seriousness, of which he himself was probably not fully aware. We can still catch echoes of this conflict in the staunch resistance which Apel puts up today against the conciliatory pragmatism of thinkers such as Richard Rorty. In Bonn the basic intention which was to shape his subsequent work was already being formed. On the one hand, not to abandon the insights of hermeneutics, always to remain sensitive to historical context and to acknowledge the strengths of the opponent's position – and yet, on the other hand, to insist on the essential vocation to philosophy, on the need to offer systematic answers to perennial questions, and to find rational forms of orientation for a life lived consciously and responsibly.

II

Apel's first book, his investigation of 'The Idea of Language in the Tradition of Humanism from Dante to Vico', which employs a broad range of historical material, and which (during a difficult phase of his life) he learned Italian to write, bears clear signs of the intellectual horizons of Bonn. But it also points towards the future, and a more systematic approach to the pragmatic dimension of language. Apel was searching for origins and precursors of the marginal figures in the philosophy of language (Vico, Hamann, Herder and Humboldt) in medieval and ancient philosophy. In doing so, he uncovered a constellation of four typical patterns of thought about language. He was interested above all in the Christian tradition of *logos* mysticism, and the Italian humanist conception of language, two approaches which were pushed aside in the modern age by the dominant currents of nominalism and the programme of a *mathesis universalis*. Using concepts derived from Scheler's theory of the forms of knowledge, Apel opposes humanistic culture and the redemptive knowledge of *logos* mysticism to nominalistic, instrumental knowledge. His quest for the traces of a marginalized way of thinking about language brought him, from an entirely different point of departure, into the vicinity of Walter Benjamin, whose work he did not know at that time. Rather, it was Heidegger who remained decisive for the thesis that 'the truth of human speech is not based primarily on a logically correct representation by means of signs of supposedly pre-given facts about the world, but on an interpretation of the world as the meaningful situation of human beings which first discloses an order of facts'[1]. However, Apel was already insisting on a transcendental-hermeneutic conception of language, which was directed against the autonomization of the world-disclosing function of language in Heidegger's history of Being. Innerworldly 'praxis' is only 'mediated' by the disclosing 'poiesis' of linguistic world-constitution. In every empirically successful interpretation a 'generally valid conceptual approach' and a 'one-sided projection of significance' must 'interpenetrate' – a thought which one can in fact already find in Rothacker.

Of course, Apel could only unfold his central idea of an interplay between a priori structures of meaning and reflection on validity after he had worked his way through analytical philosophy, and discovered Peirce as the great source of inspiration for a transformation of transcendental philosophy in the process. The idea of such a transformation had been in his mind ever since the days of his doctoral dissertation, the starting point of which was an anthropological approach to epistemological issues. During the sixties Apel was engaged in a dogged labour of reception. It is probably the rhythm of this rage for appropriation, this hermeneutic fury, which accounts for the fact that, from then on, Apel developed his most important theories in wide-ranging essays, rather than books. The book on Peirce was actually based on two large-scale introductions to collections of Peirce's essays which he edited. The book on the explanation versus *Verstehen* debate was a commentary on the Anglo-Saxon discussion of this issue. The two weighty volumes of *Transformation of Philosophy*, which made Apel's reputation in the United States and Scandinavia, as well as in Italy, Spain and Latin America, and his latest book, *Diskurs und Verantwortung*, are 'collected papers' – and yet also much more. For each individual essay is written from a systematic perspective, which it could be said to anticipate. Perhaps this is also part and parcel of a style of thought which is far more experimental in its methods than the controversial claim to 'ultimate justification' would lead one to believe. Apel tunnels again and again through the thicket of problems, yet these paths do not lead to a Hegelian synthesis, but rather out into the open. The openness is that of a striving for orientation in the style of Lessing, one which finds its fixed point of reference in regulative ideas alone.

Apel's intellectual path is marked primarily by a series of treatises. His inaugural lecture in Kiel already bore the title 'Wittgenstein and Heidegger'. Today everyone appreciates that twentieth-century philosophy has been essentially marked by the constellation of these two figures. Apel was one of the first to recognize the convergences between these initially opposed philosophies of language. But in 1962 he had to apologize for the unsettling effect of the comparison. In 1964 there followed his treatise on 'Analytical Philosophy of Language and the Problem of the *Geisteswissenschaften*', in which Apel settles accounts with the neo-positivist tradition in the philosophy of science, directing the common insights of philosophical hermeneutics and the analysis of language games against the objectivism of the unified science programme. The experience of reading this text made an enduring impression on me. It is here that the perspective of a counter-project, a theory of knowledge-guiding interests, emerges. Apel develops this into a theory of science centred on an anthropologically grounded epistemology. However, he first had to appropriate two further theoretical approaches – the praxis philosophy of the young Marx and the contemporary debate around Marxism, and – above all – the pragmatistic conception of science developed by

Peirce in his middle period. Following on from J. v. Kempski, it was Apel who made Peirce known in Germany. We have to recall the prevailing climate in German universities at the time Apel took to studying the writings of this most important of American philosophers. Outside of Frankfurt the traditional canon, which Heidegger had scarcely altered at all, was still in force. An older colleague suggested to Apel the inappropriateness of his plan to hold classes on Peirce and Wittgenstein by remarking that these figures obviously did not count amongst the 'great philosophers'.

III

The idea of a semiotic transformation of Kantian philosophy, which the younger Peirce was heading towards, must have struck like a bolt of lightning. All the loose threads could be tied together in the light of this programmatic idea. Apel seized on the three-place relation of the sign to the denoted object, the represented fact, and the interpreter, as the key to the arena of an unlimited community of communication. Within this arena the transcendental subject could be dissolved into historically situated processes of understanding, which nevertheless aim at an ideal consensus. Instead of the transcendental synthesis of apperception, the postulated agreement of a process of interpretation which stretches out into the infinite becomes the guarantor of the possible objectivity of knowledge in general. In a characteristic turn of phrase, Apel speaks of 'intersubjective understanding as the mediation of tradition within an unlimited community of interpretation'. This takes the place of the transcendental subject and mediates poiesis with praxis, genesis with validity, the context of discovery with the context of justification, the happening of meaning with the a priori of reflection on validity, the object-constitutive interests guiding knowledge with argumentation.

This breakthrough was marked by a further treatise on the question of 'Scientism or Transcendental Hermeneutics?', which first appeared in the *Festschrift* for Gadamer. It opens the way to a 'transformation of philosophy', whose architectonic Apel sketched a few years later in the introduction to the volumes which appeared under this title. Here he pursues the question of how the normative content of the epistemological reflections which Peirce developed using the model of a community of researchers could be made fruitful for the community of communicating citizens. He is concerned with how to 'treat actually existing society, which is the subject of material needs and interests, as being also the normatively ideal subject of knowledge and argumentation'.[2]

The 'a priori of the community of communication' now becomes the point of departure for a discourse ethics, which enables Apel to overcome methodological solipsism in the domain of practical philosophy. The essay of 1973 with this title marks the beginning of a series of investigations in moral theory which has continued up to the present day. Apel's work on 'The Problem of Ultimate Philosophical Justification in the Light of a Transcendental Pragmatics of Language' occupies a pre-eminent place in this series.[3] Through an engagement with critical rationalism, and in particular with Hans Albert's objections, Apel clarifies the meaning of transcendental grounding in order to show how philosophical claims to ultimate justification can be made compatible with the basic fallibilism of human knowledge. In doing so, he refers to the normative content of the pragmatic presuppositions of argumentation in general, which, he suggests, can be shown to be unavoidable. In this controversy concerning ultimate justification what is at issue is the status which the demonstration of such unavoidable presuppositions can claim. Are we confronted here with explications of meaning 'which one cannot understand without realizing that they are true'?

A fertile aspect of Apel's work is his distinction between three paradigmatic answers to the question concerning the 'privileged logos of human language'. Here the turn towards a pragmatics of language, whose targets are ontology and mentalism, becomes the key to a systematic investigation of types of rationality. This investigation sets itself the task of retrieving abandoned dimensions of the concept of reason in terms of a theory of communication. Of course, even after the linguistic turn, Apel remains a Kantian. This is true not just of his moral theory and epistemology, but also of his reflections on the philosophy of history. Even his attempt to reconstruct the evolutionary metaphysics of the later Peirce is guided by *The Critique of Judgement*.

This orientation towards Kant, the clearest and most unerring spirit of the German Enlightenment, has also made Apel a surprisingly perceptive judge in his role as a social commentator and analyst of the times. Admittedly, Apel is above all a philosopher and scholar. Despite his sense of commitment, there is a touch of the unpolitical about him. But he is also an intellectual, who has made his views clear at significant turning points in the post-war history of Germany.

IV

Even in the early 1960s there was a clear political motivation behind Apel's choice of co-ordinates for his survey of the principal trends in contemporary philosophy. In the West Apel observed a characteristic division of labour between analytical philosophy and philosophy of science, on the one hand, and existentialism and phenomenology on the other. One side was assigned responsibility for the rationality conditions of value-free, objectively valid empirical judgements, while the other took care of the sphere of private experiences and subjective decisions guided by conscience. With regard to the basic questions of practical philosophy the two orientations responded in complementary ways. Scientism leaves morality, law and politics untouched, consigning this domain of questions, regarded as irrational, or at least not capable of truth, to the decisionism of situation ethics. Behind the Iron Curtain, by contrast, there reigned a Marxist orthodoxy which completed the Western system of complementary perspectives in its own way. Marxism-Leninism contested the abstract division between objectivistic science and subjectivistic freedom, but only at the cost of a clamping together of 'Is' and 'Ought', theory and practice, science and ethics, which relied on a metaphysics of history.

Clearly, it is this characterization of contemporary philosophy which provided the backdrop for Apel's intersubjective approach to a communicative ethics. But in 1968 it also enabled Apel to take the critical intentions of the student movement seriously, and yet also warn of the danger of false totalizations. He insisted that the internal connection between knowledge and interest, science and emancipation, should not be collapsed into an identity.

If Apel fought against the dogmatism of the Left during the late 1960s, during the seventies and early eighties he had to deal with the denunciations and reproaches of the neo-conservatives. In his answer to the question, 'Is the Ethics of the Ideal Communication Community a Utopia?',[4] he achieves a convincing clarification of the relations between utopian thought, the philosophy of history, and moral theory. Discourse ethics proposes no ideal form of life; and neither does it offer a yardstick for the assessment of an intersubjectively shared life context – or an individual life-history – as a whole. Having no concept of totality at its disposal, it relies on procedural rationality. The procedure of argumentation leaves the clarification of practical questions to those concerned; but it also demands a capacity for ideal role-taking: the critique of utopian reason need not lead to the denial of unavoidable idealizations. 'In fact anyone who argues seriously must . . . assume that the conditions of an ideal community of communication . . . are in a certain sense – counterfactually – fulfilled, in other words anticipate an ideal state.'[5]

Since then the spirit of the times, and hence also the philosophical climate, has taken another turn. In one of his most recent essays Apel deals with the question: 'Back to normality? Or: is it possible that we have learned something specific from our national catastrophe?'[6] This moving document lays bare the motives for his lifelong commitment to the unconditionality and transcending force of a situated reason, motives which are deeply rooted in his life-history. Reason, on this conception, is embodied in the communicative practice of socialized individuals, who live historically, and hence suffer the blows of fate, but are not entirely helpless before them. On the one hand, Apel defends this position against neo-Aristotelian transfigurations of the fake substantiality of the merely habitual and customary; but, on the other, he is just as sharply opposed to Rorty's contextualism, and the postmodernism of Derrida and Lyotard.

In his earlier work the representatives of an older generation, Heidegger and Wittgenstein, but also Popper and Horkheimer, had been the points of reference. Apel could engage dialectically with them because he had also learned from them. Now his opponents are his peers. But this by itself would not explain the shriller tone.

The fact is that Apel finds himself confronting variations of the outlook from which he freed himself during his student years. He is faced with intensified forms of historicism. And ironically, these have emerged from a radicalization of the pragmatic turn in analytical philosophy (and structuralism) which Apel himself introduced and encouraged. It is not the *déjà vu* as such which disturbs Apel, but rather the incompatibility between the relativistic upshot of this thinking and 'what we, as contemporaries of the German catastrophe, should have learned from our particular situation'. Apel combats a historicism which has recently re-emerged under new names because this historicism 'was one of the main factors which, right at the beginning of the century in our country, led to a paralysis of the principled post-conventional moral awareness which educated people might have developed. This was another thing, I now realize, which those of us who returned from the War could clearly observe in our academic teachers after 1945.'[7]

Notes

1   K.-O. Apel, *Die Idee der Sprache* (Bonn: Bouvier Verlag, 1963), p. 28.

2 K.-O. Apel, *Transformation der Philosophie* (Frankfurt am Main: Suhrkamp, 1973), vol. 1, p. 17.

3 K.-O. Apel, 'Das Problem der philosophischen Letztbegründung im Lichte einer transzendentalen Sprachpragmatik', in B. Kanitschneider, ed., *Sprache und Erkenntnis* (Innsbruck: TAMŒ, 1976), pp. 55–82.

4 K.-O. Apel, 'Ist die Ethik der idealen Kommunikationsgemeinschaft eine Utopie?', in W. Vosskamp, ed., *Utopieforschung* (Stuttgart: Metzler, 1982), vol. 1, pp. 325–55.

5 Ibid., pp. 343ff.

6 K.-O. Apel, 'Zurück zur Normalität? – Oder könnten wir aus der nationalen Katastrophe etwas Besonderes gelernt haben?', in *Diskurs und Verantwortung* (Frankfurt am Main: Surhrkamp, 1988), pp. 370–474.

7 Ibid. pp. 386ff.

6

Israel or Athens: Where does Anamnestic Reason Belong?

Johann Baptist Metz on Unity amidst Multicultural Plurality

The thought of Johann Baptist Metz fascinates me – not least because I recognize common purposes at work, albeit across a certain distance. The fact that similar problems should arise both for the theologian and for someone who adopts the philosophical position of methodological atheism is less surprising than the parallels between the answers. I would like to offer thanks to my theological contemporary by seeking to clarify the nature of these parallels.

Metz once used his own life history to illustrate that simultaneity of the non-contemporaneous which confronts us in today's multicultural, differentiated and decentred world society:

> I come from an arch-Catholic small town in Bavaria. To come from such a place is to come from a long way away. It is as though one had been born not some fifty (or sixty-five) years ago, but rather somewhere on the twilit margins of the middle ages. I was forced to learn painfully what others, what 'society', had apparently discovered long ago ...: for example, democracy as an everyday political fact, coping with a diffuse public realm, rules for the handling of conflict, even in

Contribution to a symposium which was held on 16 June 1993 in Münster, on the occasion of Johann Baptist Metz's retirement.

family life, and so on. There was much that seemed strange, and which I still find disturbing.'[1]

Against this backdrop, Metz has always fought against a merely defensive attitude of the Catholic church to modernity, and advocated a productive participation in the processes of the bourgeois and post-bourgeois Enlightenment. If the biblical vision of salvation does not mean simply liberation from individual guilt, but also implies collective liberation from situations of misery and oppression (and thus contains a political as well as a mystical element), then the eschatological drive to save those who suffer unjustly connects up with those impulses towards freedom which have characterized modern European history.

But, of course, a blindness towards the dialectical character of enlightenment is just as fateful as an insensitivity towards the emancipatory potential of this history. The Enlightenment remained ignorant of the barbaric reverse side of its own mirror for too long. Its universal claims made it easy to overlook the particularistic kernel of its European origin. This immobilized, rigidified rationalism has been transformed into the stifling power of a capitalistic world civilization, which assimilates alien cultures and abandons its own traditions to oblivion. Christianity, which thought it could use this civilization as an 'innocent catalyst for the worldwide transmission of its message of hope', the Church which believed it could send out its missionaries in the wake of the European colonizers, participated unwittingly in this dialectic of disenchantment and loss of memory. This explains the diagnosis which Metz puts forward as a theologian, and the practical demand with which he confronts his Church.

The diagnosis runs as follows: A philosophical conception of reason derived from Greece has so alienated a Hellenized Christianity from its own origins in the spirit of Israel that theology has become insensitive to the outcry of suffering and the demand for universal justice (1 and 2). The demand can be formulated thus: A eurocentric Church, which sprang up on the ground of Hellenism, must transcend its monocultural self-conception and, remembering its

Jewish origins, unfold into a culturally polycentric global Church.

(1) *Israel versus Athens.* Metz is tireless in defending the heritage of Israel in Christianity. 'Jesus was not a Christian, but a Jew' – with this provocative statement Metz not only opposes Christian anti-semitism, he not only confronts the *ecclesia triumphans* with its deeply problematic posture as victor in the face of a blinded and humiliated synagogue;[2] above all, he rebels against the apathy of a theology which was seemingly untouched by Auschwitz.[3] This critique has an existential-practical thrust. But it also implies that, in pushing aside its Jewish origins, a Hellenized Christianity has cut itself off from the sources of anamnestic reason. It has itself become one expression of an idealistic form of reason, unburdened by fate and incapable of recollection and historical remembrance. Those who regard Christianity from an 'Augustinian' perspective as a synthesis of intellect and belief, one in which the intellect comes from Athens and the belief from Israel, 'halve' the spirit of Christianity.[4] In opposition to this division of labour between philosophical reason and religious belief, Metz insists on the rational content of the tradition of Israel; he regards the force of historical remembrance as an element of reason: 'This anamnestic reason resists the forgetting, and also the forgetting of forgetting, which lies concealed in every pure historicization of the past.'[5] From this standpoint the philosophy whose roots lie in Greece appears as the guardian of *ratio*, of the powers of understanding which only become reason through their fusion with the *memoria* which dates back to Moses and his prophetic revelation. This is why a theology which returns from its Hellenistic alienation to retrieve its own origins can claim the last word against philosophy: 'it returns to the indissoluble connection between *ratio* and *memoria* (in late modern terms: the grounding of communicative reason in anamnestic reason)'.[6]

When one considers this claim from a philosophical standpoint, it is not just the grounding role of anamnestic reason which appears contestable. The picture of the philosophical tradition is flattened out too. For this tradition cannot be subsumed under the category of Platonism. In the course of its history it has absorbed essential elements of the Judaeo-Christian heritage, it has been shaken to its very roots by the legacy of Israel. Admittedly, from Augustine via Thomas to Hegel, philosophical idealism has produced syntheses which transform the God whom Job encountered into a philosophical concept of God. But the history of philosophy is not just the history of Platonism, but also of the protests against it. These protests have been raised under the sign of nominalism and empiricism, of individualism and existentialism, of negativism or historical materialism. They can be understood as so many attempts to bring the semantic potential of the notion of a history of salvation back into the universe of grounding speech. In this way practical intuitions which are fundamentally alien to ontological thought and its epistemological and linguistic transformations have penetrated into philosophy.

Metz brings these non-Greek motifs together in the *single* focus of remembrance. He understands the force of recollection in Freud's sense as the analytical force of making conscious, but above all in Benjamin's sense as the mystical force of a retroactive reconciliation. Remembrance preserves from decay things we regard as indispensable, and yet which are now in extreme danger. This religious conception of 'salvation' certainly transcends the horizon of what philosophy can make plausible under the conditions of postmetaphysical thinking. But the concept of a saving remembrance paves the way for the disclosure of a domain of religious motives and experiences which long stood clamouring at the gates of philosophical idealism, before they were finally taken seriously, and disrupted from within a reason oriented towards the cosmos. But disruption was not the end of the story. The Greek logos has transformed itself on its path from the intellectual contemplation of the cosmos, via the self-reflection of the knowing subject, to a linguistically embodied reason. It is no longer fixated on our cognitive dealings with the world – on being as being, on the knowing of knowing, or the meaning of propositions which can be true or false. Rather the idea of a covenant which promises justice to the people of God, and to everyone who belongs to this people, a justice which extends through and beyond a history of suffering, has been taken up in the idea of a community tied by a special bond. The thought of such a community, which would entwine freedom and solidarity within the horizon of an undamaged intersubjectivity, has unfolded its explosive force even within philosophy. Argumentative reason has become receptive to the practical experiences of threatened identity suffered by those who exist historically.

Without this subversion of Greek metaphysics by notions of authentically Jewish and Christian origin, we could not have developed that network of specifically modern notions which come together in the thought of a reason which is both communicative and historically situated. I am referring to the concept of subjective freedom and the demand for equal respect for all – and specifically for the stranger in her distinctiveness and otherness. I am referring to the concept of autonomy, of a self-binding of the will based on moral insight, which depends on relations of mutual recognition. I am referring to the concept of socialized subjects, who are individuated by their life histories, and are simultaneously irreplaceable individuals and members of a community; such subjects can only lead a life which is genuinely their own through sharing in a common life with others. I am referring to the concept of liberation – both as an emancipation from degrading conditions and as the utopian project of a harmonious form of life. Finally, the irruption of historical thought into philosophy has fostered insight into the limited span of human life. It has made us more aware of the narrative structure of the histories in which we are caught up, and the fateful character of the events which confront us. This awareness includes a sense of the fallibility of the human mind, and of the contingent conditions under which even our unconditional claims are raised.

The tension between the spirit of Athens and the legacy of Israel has been worked through with no less an impact in philosophy than in theology. Philosophical thought is not exhausted by the synthetic labours of idealism, an idealism which the ecclesiastically structured, pagan Christianity of the West theologized. And this means that the critique of Hellenized Christianity does not automatically apply to argumentative reason, to the impersonal reason of the philosophers as such. Anamnesis and story-telling can also provide reasons, and so drive philosophical discourse forward, even though they cannot be decisive for it. Although profane reason must remain sceptical about the mystical causality of a recollection inspired by the history of salvation, although it cannot simply accept a general promise of restitution, philosophers need not leave what Metz calls 'anamnestic reason' entirely to the theologians. This I would like to show with reference to two themes which are of particular concern to Metz, one from the perspective of theology, and the other from that of Church politics.

(2) *The Problem of Theodicy.* The question of the salvation of those who have suffered unjustly is perhaps the most powerful moving force behind our continuing talk of God. Metz is decisively opposed to any Platonized softening of this question, which confronts Christians after Auschwitz more radically than ever.[7] In this case too, it was the conceptual tools of the Greek tradition which made it possible to separate the God of salvation from the Creator God of the Old Testament, freeing Him of responsibility for the barbarity of a sinful humankind. God Himself was not to be drawn into His creation, shot through, as it is, with suffering. Against this idealistic dilution of suffering, Metz invokes a 'culture of loss', a culture of remembrance which could keep open, without false consolation, the existential restlessness of a passionate questioning of God. An eschatologically driven anticipation, a sensitivity towards a suspended future, one which nevertheless already reaches into the present, would thereby be encouraged.[8] The biblical anticipation of the future must not, in line with Nietzsche's doctrine of the Eternal Return, be absorbed into a Greek understanding of eternity.[9]

But even this protest, which reaches inward towards the
innermost domains of religious experience, finds a parallel in
those counter-traditions of philosophical thought which
have insisted on the positivity and obstinacy of the negative,
as opposed to the Neo-Platonic conception of descending
gradations of the good and the true. In a similar way to
theologies which culminate in eschatology, this tradition,
which stretches from Jakob Böhme and Franz Baader, via
Schelling and Hegel, to Bloch and Adorno, transforms the
experience of the negativity of the present into the driving
force of dialectical reflection. Such reflection is intended to
break the power of the past over what is to come. Since
philosophy does not begin from the premise of an almighty
and just deity, it cannot make use of the question of theodicy
in its plea for a culture of loss – for a sense of what has failed
and been withheld. But in any case, philosophy today is
less concerned with the idealistic transfiguration of a
reality in need of salvation than with indifference towards a
world flattened out by empiricism, and rendered normatively
mute.

The fronts have been reversed. The historicism of
paradigms and world-pictures, now rife, is a second-level
empiricism which undermines the serious task confronting
a subject who takes up a positive or negative stance towards
validity-claims. Such claims are always raised here and now,
in a local context – but they also transcend all merely pro-
vincial yardsticks. When one paradigm or world picture is
worth as much as the next, when different discourses encode
everything that can be true or false, good or evil, in different
ways, then this closes down the normative dimension which
enables us to identify the traits of an unhappy and distorted
life. We can no longer recognize a life unworthy of human
beings, and experience the loss this involves. Philosophy, too,
pits the force of anamnesis against a historicist forgetting of
forgetting. But now it is argumentative reason itself which
reveals, in the deeper layers of its own pragmatic presuppositions, the conditions for laying claim to an unconditional
meaning. It thereby holds open the dimension of validity-
claims which transcend social space and historical time. In

this way it makes a breach in the normality of mundane events, which are devoid of any promissory note. Without this, normality would close itself hermetically against any experience of a solidarity and justice which is *lacking*. However, such a philosophy, which takes up the thought of community in the notion of a communicative, historically situated reason, cannot offer assurances. It stands under the sign of a transcendence from within, and has to content itself with the reasoned resolve of a sceptical but non-defeatist 'resistance to the idols and demons of a world which holds humanity in contempt'.

The relation between philosophy and theology shifts yet again in connection with the other theme, which crucially concerns Metz in the domain of Church politics and Church history. Here philosophy does not simply strive to appropriate semantic potentials which have been preserved in the religious tradition, as is the case with the question of theodicy. It can even assist a theology which aims to clarify the status of Christianity and the Church in the light of a pluralism of cultures and understandings of the world.[10]

(3) *The Polycentric World Church.*   Since the second Vatican Council, the Church has been confronted with the double task of opening itself up from within to the multiplicity of cultures in which Catholic Christianity has established itself, and of seeking a bold dialogue with non-Christian religions, rather than lingering in defensive apologetics. The same problem occurs in both domains: how can the Christian Church retain its identity despite its cultural multivocity; and how can Christian doctrine maintain the authenticity of its search for truth in its discursive engagement with competing images of the world? A Church which reflects on the limitations of its eurocentric history, seeking to attune Christian doctrine to the hermeneutic departure points of non-Western cultures, cannot start from the 'idea of an ahistorical, culturally unbiased and ethnically innocent Christianity'. Rather, it must remain aware both of its theological origins and of its institutional entanglement with the history of European colonialism. And a Christianity which

takes up a reflexive attitude to its own truth claims in the course of dialogue with other religions cannot rest content with an 'inconsequential or patronizing pluralism'. Rather, it must hold fast to the universal validity of its promise of salvation, whilst avoiding all assimilationist tendencies and entirely renouncing the use of force.[11]

From this perspective, the polycentric Church even seems to offer a model for dealing with the political problem of multiculturalism. In its internal relations it appears to provide the pattern for a democratic constitutional state, which allows the different life-forms of a multicultural society the right to flourish. And in its external relations such a Church could be a model for a community of nations which regulates its relations on the basis of mutual recognition. But, on closer inspection, it becomes clear that things are in fact the other way round. The idea of the polycentric Church depends in turn on insights of the European Enlightenment and its political philosophy.

Metz himself affirms the legacy of a rational conception of law which has been hermeneutically sensitized to its eurocentric limitations: Europe is

> the cultural and political home of a universalism whose kernel is strictly anti-eurocentric ... Admittedly, the universalism of the Enlightenment, which sought freedom and justice, was at first only semantically universal, and in its concrete application it has remained particularistic right up to the present day. But this universalism has also founded a new political and hermeneutic culture, one which aims at the recognition of the dignity of all human beings as free subjects. The recognition of cultural otherness must not abandon this universalism of human rights, which has been developed in the European tradition. It is this universalism which ensures that cultural pluralism does not simply collapse into a vague relativism, and that a supposed culture of sensitivity remains sensitive to issues of truth.[12]

However, Christianity cannot expect its ethically saturated conceptions of the history of salvation or of the created order to receive universal recognition *in the same sense* as a procedurally formulated theory of law and morality, which claims to ground human rights and the principles of the constitutional state with the help of a concept of procedural justice.[13] This is why even Metz understands the universality of the offer of salvation as an 'invitation' to all, which has to be practically tested, and not in terms of the claim to rational acceptability which has characterized the emergence of rational law, for example. Even the polycentric world Church remains *one* of several communities of interpretation, each of which articulates its own conception of salvation, its vision of an unspoiled life. These struggle with one another over the most convincing interpretations of justice, solidarity, and salvation from misery and humiliation. The Church must internalize this outsider perspective, make its own this gaze which is directed upon it. To achieve this it makes use of ideas which were developed by the European Enlightenment, ideas which, today, must be put into effect in democratically constituted multicultural societies, as well as in relations of recognition between the nations and cultures of this earth which are based on respect for human rights.

In multicultural societies basic rights and the principles of the constitutional state form the points of crystallization for a political culture which unites all citizens. This in turn is the basis for the coexistence of different groups and subcultures, each with its own origin and identity. The *uncoupling of these two levels of integration* is needed to prevent the majority culture from exercising a power of definition over the whole political culture. Indeed, the majority culture must subordinate itself to the political culture, and enter into a non-coercive exchange with the minority cultures. A similar situation obtains within the polycentric world Church. A shared Christian self-understanding must emerge within it, one which no longer coincides with the historically determining traditions of the West, but merely provides the backdrop which enables the Western tradition to become aware of its eurocentric limitations and peculiarities.

Another kind of hermeneutic self-reflection is required of Catholic Christianity as a whole in its relation to other religions. Here the analogy with a Western world which is coming to accept decentred and unprejudiced forms of exchange with non-Western cultures breaks down. For in this case we presuppose a common basis of human rights, which are presumed to enjoy a general and rationally motivated recognition. By contrast, in the case of the dialogical contest between religious and metaphysical world views, a common conception of the good which could play the same role as this shared legal and moral basis is lacking. This means that this contest has to be played out with a reflexive awareness that all concerned move in the same universe of discourse, and respect each other as collaborative participants in the search for ethical-existential truth. To make this possible a culture of recognition is required which takes its principles from the secularized world of moral and rational-legal universalism. In this domain, therefore, it is the philosophical spirit of political enlightenment which lends theology the concepts with which to make sense of moves towards a polycentric world Church. I say this without any intention of scoring points. For the political philosophy which performs this role is just as deeply marked by the thought of a community bound by covenant as it is by the idea of the polis. To this extent, it appeals to a biblical heritage. And it is this heritage to which Metz also appeals, when he reminds the contemporary Church that, in the name of its mission, it must 'seek freedom and justice for all', and be guided by 'a culture of the recognition of the other in his otherness'.[14]

Notes

1   J. B. Metz, *Unterbrechungen* (Gütersloh: Güterloher Verlaghaus Mohn, 1980), p. 13.

2   K. J. Kuschel, ed., *Welches Christentum hat Zukunft? Dorothee Sölle und Johann Baptist Metz im Gespräch* (Stuttgart: Kreuz-Verlag, 1990), pp. 23ff.

3   J. B. Metz, *Jenseits bürgerlicher Religion* (Munich: Kaiser, 1980).

4   J. B. Metz, 'Anamnestic Reason', in Axel Honneth et al., eds, *Cultural-Political Interventions in the Unfinished Process of*

Enlightenment (Cambridge, Mass. and London: MIT Press, 1992), pp. 189–94.

5   J. B. Metz, 'Die Rede von Gott angesichts der Leidens-geschichte der Welt', in *Stimmen der Zeit*, 5, 1992, p. 24.

6   Ibid.

7   J. B. Metz, 'Im Angesicht der Juden. Christliche Theologie nach Auschwitz', in *Concilium*, 20, 1984, pp. 382–9.

8   See 'Die Rede von Gott angesichts der Leidensgeschichte der Welt'. M. Theunissen speaks in this context of a 'proleptic future'. See 'Communicative Freedom and Negative Theo-logy', pp. 90–111 in this volume.

9   M. Theunissen, *Negative Theologie der Zeit* (Frankfurt am Main: Suhrkamp, 1991), p. 368.

10 J. B. Metz, 'Theologie im Angesicht und vor dem Ende der Moderne', in *Concilium*, 20, 1984, pp. 14–18.

11 J. B. Metz, 'Im Aufbruch zu einer kulturell polyzentrischen Weltkirche', in F. X. Kaufmann, J. B. Metz, *Zukunftsfähigkeit* (Freiburg: Herder, 1987), pp. 93–115.

12 J. B. Metz, 'Perspektiven eines multikulturellen Christen-tums', MS, Dec. 1992.

13 John Rawls, *A Theory of Justice* (Cambridge, Mass.: Harvard University Press, 1971). J. Habermas, *Between Facts and Norms* (Cambridge: Polity, 1996).

14 Metz, *Zukunftsfähigkeit*, p. 118.

7

Communicative Freedom and Negative Theology

Questions for Michael Theunissen

The quiet radicality of Michael Theunissen's thought derives from his simultaneous openness to Kierkegaard and to Marx. Theunissen responds to the two creative minds who – more radically than all others – were marked by their engagement with the speculative thought of Hegel. This is why he has paid special attention to the two styles of thought which have brought Kierkegaard and Marx back to philosophical life in our century: existential ontology and Hegelian Marxism. He engages with both traditions by returning to their original points of inspiration: in his view, the insights of the authentic Kierkegaard and a critically appropriated Marx are superior to those of Heidegger and Sartre, or Horkheimer and Adorno.[1] In this project Theunissen is aided by a turn towards the theory of communication which he made early on in his career. He emphasizes the relevance of the second person – the other in the role of 'Thou' – in contrast to a subject–object relation defined by the attitudes of first and third person.

The dialogical encounter with an other whom I address, and whose answer lies beyond my control, first opens the intersubjective space in which the individual can become an authentic self. Theunissen developed his philosophy of

Essay first published in *Dialektischer Negativismus*, ed. E. Angehrn et al., 1992.

dialogue through a critical engagement with the transcendental theory of intersubjectivity, as developed from Husserl to
Sartre. It is inspired not just by Buber's 'theology of the
between', but also draws directly on theological motifs.
Indeed, Theunissen understands that 'middle' of the intersubjective space which the dialogical encounter discloses,
and which in turn enables self and other to become themselves through dialogue, as the 'kingdom of God' which
precedes and founds the existing sphere of subjectivity.
Referring to Luke 17: 21 – 'the kingdom of God is among
you' – Theunissen declares: 'It exists *between* the human
beings who are called to it, as a present future.' Throughout
his career, Theunissen has tried to retrieve the content of this
crucial statement in *philosophical* terms. For 'presumably the
reality as which the between discloses itself to dialogical
thinking in a theological perspective is the only side of the
kingdom of God that philosophy can catch a glimpse of at all:
the side not of "grace", but of the "will". The will to dialogical self-becoming belongs to the striving after the kingdom
of God, whose future coming is promised in the present love
of human beings for one another.'[2]

Later in his career, Theunissen sought to integrate this
theological motif into a critical social theory with the aid of
the concept of 'communicative freedom'. His aim was to
make Kierkegaard compatible with Marx. He has not evaded
the decision which this project eventually required: the choice
between a materialistic and a theological reading of reconciliation. He has always preferred the proleptic appearance of
an *eschaton* which can instil *confidence* into the present to a
rationally *fortified* transcendence from within. But, in his view,
even this option can be philosophically grounded. This is the
claim that I would like to test in what follows. Theunissen
finds the possibility of such a grounding in Kierkegaard, and he
seems to find it, in particular, in an aspect of Fichte's theory
which was taken up by Kierkegaard. Of course, Theunissen
has no wish to hide behind the authority of the author of *The
Sickness unto Death*. But Kierkegaard's arguments do provide
the impetus behind Theunissen's negativistic grounding of an
authentic selfhood.

I would first like to outline the claim that essential contents of the Christian gospel of salvation can be justified under the conditions of postmetaphysical thinking. I will then discuss the arguments which Theunissen employs in his effort to satisfy this claim by pursuing 'the paths of philosophical thought which are still viable today'. My critical queries do not affect my sense of solidarity with a remarkable enterprise, one with which I feel closely allied in its practical motivation and intentions.

I

In the history of Western thought since Augustine, Christianity has entered into many kinds of symbiotic relationship with the metaphysical tradition stemming from Plato. Along with theologians such as Jürgen Moltmann and Johann Baptist Metz,[3] Theunissen has sought to retrieve the original eschatological content of a Christianity freed from its Hellenistic shell. The kernel thus retrieved is a radically historical mode of thought which is incompatible with essentialist conceptions: 'It is the domination of what is past over what is to come which results in the compulsive character of a reality in need of salvation. This reality takes the form of a universal pattern of compulsion because, within it, the future is constantly overwhelmed by the past.'[4] In Theunissen this sentence has a precise meaning which extends beyond Adorno's 'negative dialectics':

> If it is the domination of the past which causes human beings to sink into the helplessness of an incapacity to act, then what awakens them from this helplessness is the liberating action of God. Existence within time, which the metaphysical tradition deriving from Plato viewed under the negative aspect of the mutable, acquires the positive shape of the alterable.[5]

However, what distinguishes Theunissen's position from that of theologians with similar aims is the claim that he can achieve their common goal with non-theological means.

Indeed, Theunissen borrows these means from the basic repertoire of metaphysical concepts bequeathed by the very Platonism which is to be overcome. In so doing, he abandons the careful distinction between those aspects of 'grace' under which the kingdom of God is disclosed only to theologians, and of 'will' under which it also appears to philosophers. He seems confident that he can close the gap between the appeal to a reality experienced in faith, and the power to convince of philosophical reasons. What is more, he thinks he can do so with arguments.

After the catastrophes of our century, Benjamin's intuition that the bad continuity of all previous history must be broken apart – the cry of the tortured creature, that 'everything must be different' – undoubtedly has a more than merely suggestive force. Today we are confronted on all sides by the regressions which the collapse of the Soviet empire has triggered. In the face of these phenomena, the impulse to *rebel* against the domination of the past over the future,[6] even the imperative to burst the shackles of the fatal return of the same, seems to require no extensive justification: 'Benjamin has evoked the unutterable sadness of a history which has congealed into nature. History would first come into being only if time itself could become other than it is.'[7] But what sense are we to make of such an expectation? Do we regard it as the prospect of an event yet to occur, as trust in a promised reversal, or as hope for the success of an enterprise which enjoys divine favour, perhaps even grace? Or is the semantic potential of the anticipation of salvation intended only to hold open a *dimension*, one which, even in profane times, offers us a criterion by which to orient ourselves towards what is better *in given circumstances*, and from which we can draw encouragement?

The hope that one's own activity is not a fortiori meaningless can be wrested from pessimism, and indeed despair, with more or less valid reasons. But such rationally motivated encouragement should not be confused with an existential confidence which emerges out of the totalized scepticism of a despair which is turned against itself. The *hope* that 'everything within time will be different' must be distinguished from the *faith* that 'time itself will be different'. The ambiguous formula of a 'becoming other of time' [*Anderswerden der Zeit*] conceals this difference between trust in an eschatological turning of the world, and the profane expectation that our praxis in the world, despite everything, may help to bring about a shift towards a better state of things. On this side of a *spes fidei* nourished by the Kierkegaardian dialectics of despair, there is room for fallible hope, instructed by a sceptical, but non-defeatist conception of reason. This *docta spes* is not to be despised, even though it can sometimes be devastated. Presumably, Theunissen would not deny the distinction, but he would hold fast to the task of showing philosophically why profane hope must be anchored in eschatological hope.

In his most recent publication, Theunissen names three paths of philosophical thought which he regards as still viable today. Philosophy can entrust itself with the critical appropriation of the history of metaphysics as a whole; it can make a contribution to reflection on the specialized sciences, and it can even retrieve, from its postmetaphysical vantage point, metaphysical contents of the tradition which resist scientific objectification. According to this programme, philosophy first follows the path of historical self-reflection, in order to secure its hold on the concepts which it then unfolds systematically in its passage through the sciences, and in the space beyond them.[8] Thus, the themes which concern Theunissen from a historical standpoint already reveal a systematic intention. Under the title 'communicative freedom' he analyses the relation between subjectivity and intersubjectivity in an exploration of Hegel's *Logic*. And with one eye on the *proleptic future* of a Christian promise of salvation which reaches into the present, he analyses the forgetfulness of time characteristic of metaphysical thought from Parmenides through to Hegel. From both perspectives Theunissen traces the ontologization of theology, in other words a Hellenization of Christianity which covers over the redemptive content of radically historical thinking. Like Heidegger, Theunissen is striving for a deconstruction of the history of metaphysics. But the aim he has in mind is not the 'archaeological' one of leaping out of modernity back towards a time before Jesus and Socrates. Theunissen's goal, rather, is a philosophically grounded negative theology. The task of this theology is to recall a disintegrated modernity from its dispersal, re-sensitizing it to a message of salvation which has become unintelligible.

II

Theunissen applies a hypothesis to Hegel's *Logic*, which – in its own way – summarizes the history of Western metaphysics. It is one which he derives from post-Hegelian philosophy: 'Hegel bases his whole logic on the hypothesis that everything which exists can only be itself in relation, and – ultimately – *as* the relation to its other.'[9] Theunissen opposes the being-for-itself of subjectivity to this self-relation which realizes itself in the relation to the other. True selfhood expresses itself as communicative freedom – as being-with-*oneself*-in-the-other; love – being-with-oneself-in-the-*other* – stands in a complementary relation to this. The interrelation – or better, coincidence – of freedom and love defines the unimpaired intersubjectivity of a relation of reciprocal recognition. In such a relation one partner is not the limit of the other's freedom, but the very condition of the other's successful selfhood. And the communicative freedom of one individual cannot be complete without the realized freedom of all others. This notion of a solidaristic and non-compulsive form of socialization enables Theunissen to give Hegel's concrete universal a dialogical structure, one which can be turned against Hegel himself with critical intent. 'Abstraction' then comes to mean an 'indifference towards what is other' which neutralizes the 'relation to the other'. Because it impedes communicative freedom, this indifference comes in turn to signify domination. Read from the standpoint of a theory of communication, Hegel's dialectic acquires a new meaning as a critique of *domination*.

Theunissen argues with Hegel against Hegel. He highlights the passages where Hegel deviates from the path of a dialectical investigation of the 'praxis of speaking with one another', and neglects the obvious dimension of the pragmatics of language for the sake of a logical analysis of the 'mere judgement or proposition'.[10] Hegel's logical and semantic restriction of his investigation bolsters the arrogance of the model of reflection, which privileges the being-with-oneself of the epistemic self-relation over the relation to the other. Whereas communicative freedom would foster the reciprocal recognition of difference and otherness, the reflection model enforces unity and totalization.[11]

Theunissen also opposes the affirmative traits of the theodicy concealed in dialectical logic, with its equation of the real and the rational. Hegel's concept of the 'untrue' effaces the difference between the contentless, and that which has not yet developed. Theunissen seeks to restore this difference with the aid of Marx's distinction between presentation and critique. The dissolution of objective illusion need not always disclose the truth of a new positivity; it often functions destructively, in the sense that it unmasks the truth *about* something.[12] Significantly, this aspect of his thought already highlights what Theunissen, despite all his criticisms, is unwilling to criticize in Hegel – the concept of the absolute.

There is a plausible claim to be made that Hegel's concept of determinate negation assumes a unity of presentation [*Darstellung*] and critique which blunts the critical edge of presentation. But Theunissen reduces this to a merely methodological question, even though, in Hegel, the unity of presentation and critique is grounded in the substantive assumption that the world-process as a whole has a logical structure. Theunissen does not touch on this metaphysical core of the problem. He does not consider the difficulty that no pathogenesis of history can arise from the orthogenesis of nature, if the historical process has the same logical form as that of events in nature. His critique of Hegel does not extend to Hegel's *totalization* of being-with-oneself-in-the-other, which assumes that the world *as a whole* is communicatively constituted. The idea of the unity of the relation to self and the relation to the other guides the *whole movement* of Hegel's logic, and extends to embrace a reality which is understood *entirely* in intersubjective terms. This idea is in no sense restricted to the sphere of interpersonal relations. Theunissen accepts this, although he stresses that reading the *Logic* as a universal theory of communication should make clear that 'the structure it reveals finds its appropriate realization only in the relation of human subjects to each other'.[13] In other words, Theunissen does not dissent from the metaphysical assumption that the basic structure of being-with-oneself-in-the-other, which is derived from the process of dialogical understanding, extends beyond the horizon of the lifeworld to embrace the world as a whole.

This is because he is convinced that every interpersonal relation is embedded in a relation to the radically Other, which precedes the relation to the concrete other. This radically Other embodies an absolute freedom which we must presuppose in order to explain how our communicative freedom is possible at all: 'for nothing can be absolute unless it can release the other out of itself, in such a way that the freedom of the other is also its own freedom from and towards itself.'[14] This conception can be traced back to elements of Jewish and Protestant mysticism, which have been passed down through Swabian Pietism: God's freedom is confirmed by the fact that He is able to produce an equally free alter ego out of Himself. In handing over to human beings the freedom to fall short of – and to struggle to achieve – selfhood through their own efforts, God withdraws from the world. God is present in the history of human communication only as an enabling and guiding structure of reconciliation – and indeed in the form of a promise, the 'anticipatory' present of a fulfilled future.[15]

As this shows, a systematic appropriation of the history of metaphysics can reveal problematic issues which are perhaps not yet outdated. But can it abolish our distance from the solutions which were proposed in the language of metaphysics? Even a reading of the 'Logic of the Notion' in terms of a theory of communication can, at best, make us *familiar* with the idea that the communicative freedom of being-with-oneself-in-the-other presupposes the absolute freedom of the radically Other. In the last analysis, it still remains undecided how this potential contained in the structure of undistorted communication is to be understood. Should we see it as an idealizing excess, which requires an ability to transcend the given context on the part of those involved in communicative action *themselves?* Or should we view it as the irruption of an anticipatory event of communicative liberation, which demands *self-abandonment* on the part of those left to make sense of their own freedom? If we assume that God has withdrawn into the transcendent moment of the structure of linguistic understanding, and has entrusted the historical process to His creatures, who are condemned to communicative freedom, then the very myth of a self-limiting God must eventually succumb to their secularizing labours. But if God *remains* the only guarantee within history that the ceaseless, nature-bound cycles of history – dominated, as it is, by the past – can be broken, then the notion of an absolute which is presupposed in every successful act of mutual understanding is left without an adequate philosophical explanation. This task cannot be carried out by means of a destruction of the history of metaphysics.

III

This is why Theunissen tries to achieve a postmetaphysically oriented grounding of the metaphysical content of communicative freedom. He unfolds his argument with reference to the text *The Sickness unto Death*.

(1)   First of all, Theunissen distinguishes his 'negativistic' procedure from a 'normativistic' one. In modern times, since the abandonment of the concepts of substance and essence which anchored what ought to be in the order of things, the architectonics of reason has replaced objective teleology. This means that normative contents can only be derived

reconstructively from the necessary subjective conditions for the objective validity of our experiences and judgements. They can no longer be derived ontologically from being itself. Of course, the shift from the paradigm of consciousness to the paradigm of mutual understanding achieved by the pragmatics of language has given yet another new direction to the investigation of normatively significant transcendental conditions. Now it is the fact of successful intersubjective communication which requires explanation. In the general and unavoidable pragmatic presuppositions of communication, we discover the counter-factual content of idealizations which all subjects must accept in so far as they orient their action towards validity-claims at all. The non-arbitrary character of the *broadly* normative content of the unavoidable presuppositions of communication can be established neither ontologically, nor epistemologically. In other words, it cannot be shown with reference to the purposive character of being, or with reference to the rational endowments of subjectivity. It can only be made plausible through the lack of alternatives to a practice in which communicatively socialized subjects always already find themselves engaged. I have adopted this formal-pragmatic approach in my own work, in order to reveal a rational potential in the validity-basis of action oriented towards mutual understanding. This rational potential can provide the normative basis for a critical theory of society.[16]

Theunissen rejects this 'normativism', but not because he detects in it the metaphysical trace of essential determinations and objective teleology.[17] On the contrary, the 'negativism' which is supposed to guide his own procedure shifts the normative content back into the ontical domain, albeit through an inversion of the 'ought' inherent in being. Whereas the logical operation of negation applies to the affirmative validity-claim which a second person raises for his utterance, 'ontic negativity' is an intrinsic property of whatever we evaluate negatively: 'What we mean by the "negative" here is that with which we do not agree, or that which we do not (cannot) will to exist. In this (ontological) sense, it ought not to be.'[18] Admittedly, the negativity of that which should not be, or the objectively untrue, is no longer related, like objective teleology, to entities in the world, or the cosmos of beings as a whole. In line with an inverted philosophy of history, the constitution of the historical world in which human beings live and suffer becomes negative. The negativity of the constitution of being is the *experienced* negativity of a lifeworld or life history. For this reason, the investigation is supposed to begin from the 'negativity of the existing world' and derive the yardstick of critique from this negativity. Theunissen's justification for this 'negativistic' procedure is that the pervasive pathology of the prevailing state of the world has long since corrupted the criteria for an *innocent* distinction between health and sickness, truth and untruth, idea and appearance. Once the sickness of the healthy is revealed, then any diagnosis carried out in the light of an unquestioned assumption of normality falls prey to the hermeneutics of suspicion.

(2) Beginning from Marx and Kierkegaard, there are ways of trying to demonstrate negatively that communicative freedom harbours a potential for betterment and reconciliation. One can point to the social *alienation* experienced in societies that have undergone capitalist rationalization, and the existential *despair* of the isolated individual in a secularized modernity. To a large extent, Theunissen has left the first path for his pupils to follow;[19] he has concentrated on working out an argument which Kierkegaard introduces for the identity of belief in God and being-a-self.[20] The reconstruction of this line of argument characterizes the phenomenon of despair in the first instance as ontic negativity. Despair radicalizes the negativity of an inadequate or oppressive state of affairs, which is experienced in boredom, care, anxiety and melancholy, into a deficient mode of being as such. Despair reveals the failure of a human life as a whole. As a form of what should simply not be the case, despair reveals something about its unrealized opposite – successfully 'being-a-self'. This is why the range of phenomena associated with despair can serve as Kierkegaard's raw material, enabling him to start his analysis guided by the notion of a sickness of the self, even before he has attained a normative conception of the self.

After this methodological clarification, Theunissen approaches the phenomenon of despair with a transcendental question: 'How is the human being constituted, and how is his self to be conceived, if we are to make sense of the despair which he experiences as the reality of the self?'[21] This question immediately implies a second question: how is selfhood possible, given that it has to be presupposed in the process of liberation from the ever-present pull of despair? What makes selfhood possible as the process of the 'constant annihilation of the possibility of despair'? The answer, according to Kierkegaard, is that the being-a-self of the self can only succeed when, in its self-positing, it relates itself to another through whom it was itself posited. Human beings can only escape despair when the self is grounded 'transparently in the power which has posited it'. This thesis is justified with reference to the existential dialectic of two basic forms of despair. In our despondent not-wanting-to-be-ourselves, we experience the fact that we cannot get free of ourselves, that we are condemned to freedom and must posit ourselves. But in the subsequent stage of desperately wanting-to-be-ourselves, we experience the uselessness of our determined efforts to posit ourselves through our own power alone. We can only finally escape the despair of this *defiant* self-grounding when we become aware of the finitude of our freedom, and thereby of our dependence on an infinite power: 'The preconditions of not being in despair are also the preconditions of successfully being a self. The fact that human beings, in positing themselves, must accept the priority of the Other who has established them as self-positing, is thus the very definition of being a self.'[22]

(3) Theunissen regards this existential-dialectical demonstration of the grounding of being-a-self in faith as 'an argument which is difficult to controvert'. But even on his own account this argument requires a supplement which highlights the communicative structure of the capacity to be a self. Up till now, the explication of the fundamental structure of being-with-oneself-in-the-other has stated no more than the following: a human being, with her finite freedom, can only be herself when she frees herself from a narcissistic-

ally enclosed selfhood through recognition of the absolute
freedom of God, and returns to herself from the infinite
distance of a communication through faith with the sheerly
Other. This explanation remains inadequate with regard to
that trivial, innerworldly aspect of being-with-oneself-in-the-
other which nonetheless offers us our primary encounter
with communicative freedom. Theunissen criticizes the
peculiar worldlessness of selfhood, which Kierkegaard
emphasized in his negative treatment of despair. 'Of course,
like Hegel, Kierkegaard understands selfhood as being-with-
oneself-in-the-other, but on his account the other is found
exclusively in God, and no longer in the world.'[23] The mere
reflexivity of relating oneself to one's relation-to-self must be
incorporated into the *intersubjectivity* of a surrender to the
other: 'In love, we experience a spontaneous opening up of
that primordial dimension of human freedom which faith has
also revealed itself to be.'[24]

Thus Theunissen returns from a reconstructed Kierkegaard
to a Hegel construed from the standpoint of a theory of
communication. He grounds the complementary relation of
love and communicative freedom in the absolute freedom
and love of God. For 'all genuine love for other human
beings . . . [is] . . . love of God'.

IV

Even if we go along with this extension of the existential-
dialectical approach towards a theory of communication, a
question still remains. It is not obvious that the Kierkegaardian argument which Theunissen so carefully reconstructs,
and which must bear the real burden of proof, can deliver
what it is supposed to deliver. The argument is supposed to
show that, in order to be fully herself, a human being must
assume that an empowerment through the absolute freedom
of God has preceded her own communicative freedom. My
reservations concern both the negativistic procedure, and the
transfer of transcendental questions into the domain of
anthropological facts.[25]

Naturally, we prefer not to be in despair. But our rejection of the negatively valued phenomenon of despair does not provide us with any positive distinguishing feature of the mere absence of the phenomenon – in other words, of not being in despair. This state may be a necessary condition of authentic selfhood, but it is not in itself a sufficient one. The *overcoming* of despair can only indicate a *successful* achievement of authentic selfhood if, *right from the beginning*, we establish a strong internal link between the phenomenon of despair and the mode of wanting-to-be-a-self. Further-more, this has to be done through the use of clinical concepts such as psychic health. But then it is the normatively laden hermeneutic pre-understanding which discloses despair as a symptom of sickness. An interpretation which takes this approach can no longer be characterized as purely negativistic.

Moreover, the transcendental question of the conditions of selfhood could only be applied to an existential mood such as despairingly wanting-to-be-oneself, if the universality and irreplaceability of this 'fundamental state of mind' could be assumed. The analysis of transcendental conditions is only meaningful with regard to activities of a general nature, for which there are no functional equivalents. The transcen-dentalization of facts or existential experiences of the self has the unfortunate consequence of requiring us to attribute a world-constituting status to something which occurs within the world. If the transcendental grounding of selfhood as not-being-in-despair is to succeed, then a despondent wanting-to-be-oneself must belong to the human condition, and represent something like a general anthropological fact. We must also be able to rule out the possibility that different phenomena of a non-despondent wanting-to-be-oneself might appear as candidates for an analogous grounding of selfhood.

But there is a further issue The real difficulty arises from the fact that what is to be explained, the point of departure for the question concerning conditions of possibility, must somehow already be a proven result. Transcendental questions are posed with reference to *substantiated* results,

which fulfil corresponding conditions of validity: true statements, grammatical sentences, binding speech acts, illuminating theories, successful works of art and literature, and so
on. From Theunissen's perspective, Kierkegaard, too, is
inquiring into the conditions of possibility – if not of an
achieved result – then of the process of successfully becoming a self. How is selfhood possible as the process of coming
to terms with a despair which arises again and again? But in
the case of Kant's question concerning the possibility of
objective experience, it is a matter of rendering transparent
the genesis of an accomplishment which is already accepted
as valid, whose outcome we *encounter* as a fact in need of
explanation, and which we can reproduce in as many exam-
ples as we like. But Kierkegaard starts from a very different
kind of fact – from a despondent *wanting*-to-be-oneself
which leaves open the question of success. What Kierkegaard
wants to make transparent in its genesis has still not been
validated. For the normal state is sickness, and only this
provides the backdrop against which a 'healthy' kind of
human existence can be delineated. The mode of successfully
being a self can only be employed in a *hypothetical* way in the
transcendental clarification of its conditions of possibility.
Under these premises, faith could only be justified in
functional terms, as the appropriate means of achieving the
implied goal of wanting-to-be-oneself. But a functional argument is not sufficient to support the thesis which Theunissen
wants to ground by means of Kierkegaard's argument,
namely that: 'The emergence, out of freedom *from* oneself,
of freedom *towards* oneself occurs at the deepest level of
faith, as the communicative genesis of selfhood.'[26] A faith
which is functionally grounded destroys itself.

Theunissen overestimates the scope of the argument
which he reconstructs from Kierkegaard. Even when he has
recourse to the horizontal axis of interpersonal relations to
supplement vertical communication with God, this does not
bring the benefit he expects. It is true that the standpoint
of formal-pragmatic analysis also regards those involved in
communicative action as called on to achieve a transcendence from within, since, with every successful act of

communication, they must orient themselves towards transcending validity-claims. But this modest truth is not enough for Theunissen. He would like to interpret successful acts of understanding in terms of a transcendence irrupting into history, the promissory presence of an absolute power which first makes our finite freedom possible. He repeatedly devises new arguments aimed at transforming Kierkegaard's 'leap of faith' into a transition which can be rationally thought through.[27] For Theunissen is too much of a philosopher to accept the statement which Dostoyevsky made (in a letter to Natalya Vonwisin dated 20 February 1854): 'If someone could prove to me that Christ is outside the truth, and if the truth really did exclude Christ, then I should prefer to stay with Christ and not truth.' Theunissen believes he has *philosophical reasons* capable of justifying and strengthening his commitment to a de-Hellenized *eschaton*. I am unable to accept these reasons, though I do accept that there can be rational motives for the conviction that one has such reasons.

V

One motive for such confidence can be found in the harsh polemic which Theunissen directs against the formalism of ethical thinking based on the moral 'ought'.[28] In this he follows Hegel's critique of Kant. Freedom in the moral sense of self-determination is manifested in the free will; and Kant terms the will 'free' when it lets itself be bound by moral insights and does what is in the equal interest of all. The task of moral theory is to clarify how correct moral judgements are possible. Basically, it is we who entrust ourselves with the rational resolution of practical questions. Since the ideas of justice and solidarity are inherently woven into communicative forms of socialization, discourse ethics seeks to clarify this fact in terms of the general pragmatic presuppositions of communicative action and argumentation. Theunissen renews Hegel's criticism of the impotence of this weak conception of morality. In reality, moral insights must secure the collaboration of concrete life forms, if they are to be practically effective.[29] For they can only appeal to the capacities of human beings who *need encouragement*, and who realize that, for all their dependence on favourable circumstances, they must ultimately rely on themselves.

The situation is different in the case of freedom in the ethical sense of self-realization. This is manifested in a conscious conduct of life, whose success cannot be attributed to the autonomy of finite beings alone. Theunissen seems to assume that ethics should explain the successful achievement of selfhood in the same way that moral theory explains how we have always already entrusted ourselves with making correct moral judgements. But in this case, 'ethics' would have to name a source of authority which could guarantee the possibility of an unspoiled life for everyone. For only thus could we assume the *capacity* to be a self as a transcendental fact, comparable to the ability to make corrrect moral judgements. But an unspoiled life does not lie within our power in the same way as correct moral judgement and action. Hence, when a similar transcendental question concerning conditions of possibility is posed with respect to successfully achieved selfhood, the fact that such selfhood is not entirely at our command requires it to be guaranteed by another power. This problematic issue makes clear why, even disregarding other considerations, Theunissen's argumentative strategy prevents him from renouncing the relation to an absolute freedom. But Kant realized that the logic of *this* kind of inquiry allows us to justify God as a practical postulate, at best. Our need to avoid falling into despair, and to hold open the prospect of happiness even under the domination of time, does not provide sufficient grounds for philosophy to announce a *dependable* outcome.

These considerations at least make the disputed point clear. Under the conditions of postmetaphysical thinking, can we answer the question of the good life – in modern guise, the question of successfully achieved selfhood – in a more than simply formal way? For example, can we provide a philosophical adumbration of the gospel message?

I discern a further motive for Theunissen's positive answer to this question in his selective description of communication. For the philosophy of dialogue simply exchanges the subject–object relation – the relation between first and third person which is privileged by the philosophy of consciousness – for the relation between first and second person. It does not exhaust the full meaning of the system of personal pronouns. The epistemic self-relation was initially envisaged as a form of self-observation. This reflection model comes to be replaced by a communicatively mediated self-relation which is structured in terms of the connection between I and Thou. It is conceived as a practical self-relation, as love or as communicatively mediated freedom, depending on whether the second or the first person is emphasized (in other words, as being-with-oneself-*in-the-other*, or being-*with-oneself*-in-the-other). But this approach elevates a special case, reciprocal ethical self-understanding concerning who one is and would like to be, to the status of the prototype of processes of reaching agreement in general. Indeed, the philosophy of dialogue directs attention away from the structure of the process of reaching agreement as such, and displaces it onto the existential experience of self achieved by the participants, an experience which is *brought about* by successful communication. For the sake of pure intersubjectivity, it overlooks the relation to the objective world built into the structure of reaching-agreement-concerning-something. It neglects what communication is *about*. As a result, the dimension of the validity of truth-claims is closed off in favour of the dimension of authenticity. And even this dimension can only be held open against the narcissistic pull of a worldless discourse of self-exploration by recourse to a universal which is introduced through the back door, as it were, and which is said to make communication possible in the first place.

This is why, as long ago as 1969, Theunissen made a plea for an 'absolute objectivity, which reaches beyond intersubjectivity and is the subject's ultimate ground'.[30] In a later study, devoted to the 'obscure' relation of universality and intersubjectivity, he repeats the thesis that 'in our self-realization, we have to achieve universality'.[31] Theunissen believes he cannot afford to give up the fundamentalistic connection to an authority which guarantees objectivity and truth, because otherwise 'intersubjectivity...is only an extension of subjectivity'.[32] But such a corrective ceases to be necessary if we free the structure of reaching-an-agreement-concerning-something from its restriction to the 'other'. This is a restriction which typifies the philosophy of dialogue. If we *integrate* the stance towards something in the objective world with the performative attitudes of the first- and second-person participants, then the complementarity of communicative freedom and love affirmed by Theunissen also disintegrates. Communicative freedom then takes on the profane, but by no means contemptible form of the responsibility of communicatively acting subjects. It consists in the fact that participants can orient themselves towards questions of validity. They do this when they raise validity-claims, when they take positive or negative stances towards the validity-claims of others, and when they accept illocutionary obligations.

The interplay of finite subjects' communicative freedom opens an horizon which *also* enables us to experience the domination of the past over the future as a mark of the wounded history of both societies and persons. Whether we adapt cynically to this reality, submit to it with melancholy, or despair over it and over ourselves, is revealed by those phenomena in which Theunissen rightly takes such an intense interest. But the philosopher will give a *different* description of these phenomena from the theologian, even though it need by no means be a discouraging one. Reflections from damaged life are equally the concern of both; but once theological and philosophical discourses have become disentangled,[33] such reflections are distinguished in terms of their status and their claims. Philosophical discourses can be recognized by the fact that they stop short of the rhetoric of fate and promised salvation.

Of course, if anomalies become the norm, which is something Theunissen takes for granted has occurred, then the phenomena begin to get blurred. In this case, to discern the relevant phenomena at all, it may be appropriate to do philosophy in the mode – but only *in the mode* – of negative theology.

Notes

1   On Heidegger, see M. Theunissen, *Negative Theologie der Zeit* (Frankfurt am Main: Suhrkamp, 1991), pp. 343ff. On Horkheimer, see M. Theunissen, 'Society and History: A Critique of Critical Theory', in P. Dews, ed., *Habermas: A Critical Reader* (Blackwell: Oxford, 1999), pp. 241–71.
2   Michael Theunissen, *The Other: Studies in the Social Ontology of Husserl, Heidegger, Sartre and Buber* (Cambridge, Mass.: MIT Press 1984), p. 383 (trans. altered by PD).
3   See J. B. Metz, 'Anamnestic Reason', in A. Honneth et al., eds, *Cultural-Political Interventions in the Unfinished Project of Enlightenment* (Cambridge, Mass. and London: MIT Press, 1992), pp. 189–94.
4   *Negative Theologie der Zeit*, p. 370.
5   Ibid., pp. 370ff.
6   Cf. Jürgen Habermas, *The Past as Future*, tr. Max Pensky (Lincoln: University of Nebraska Press).
7   *Negative Theologie der Zeit*, p. 65.
8   Theunissen, 'Möglichkeiten des Philosophierens heute', in ibid., pp. 13–36.
9   Theunissen, *Sein und Schein* (Frankfurt am Main: Suhrkamp, 1978), p. 28.
10 Ibid., pp. 468ff.
11 Ibid., pp. 455ff.
12 Ibid., pp. 70ff, 88ff.
13 Ibid., p. 463.
14 Ibid., pp. 326ff.
15 This explains Theunissen's interest in the broader theme of the forgetfulness of time in metaphysical thought. In this context, Theunissen is concerned to develop an adequate concept of the futuristic presence of the 'time of eternity'. See Theunissen, 'Zeit des Lebens', in *Negative Theologie der Zeit*, pp. 299–320; also Theunissen, 'Metaphysics' Forgetfulness of Time: On the Controversy over Parmenides Frag. 8,5', in A. Honneth et al., eds, *Philosophical Interventions in the Unfinished Project of Enlightenment* (Cambridge, Mass. and London: MIT Press, 1992), pp. 3–28.

16 J. Habermas, 'Handlungen, Sprechakte, sprachlich vermittelte Interaktion und Lebenswelt', in *Nachmetaphysiches Denken* (Frankfurt am Main: Suhrkamp, 1988), pp. 63ff.

17 M. Theunissen, 'Zwangszusammenhang und Kommunikation', in *Kritische Gesellschaftstheorie* (Berlin: de Gruyter, 1981), pp. 41ff, and esp. pp. 53ff.

18 M. Theunissen, 'Negativität bei Adorno', in L. v. Friedeburg, J. Habermas, eds, *Adorno-Konferenz 1983*, Frankfurt am Main 1983, pp. 41ff. My bracketed interpolations.

19 Cf. most recently the interesting work by G. Lohmann, *Indifferenz und Gesellschaft* (Frankfurt am Main: Suhrkamp, 1991).

20 M. Theunissen, *Das Selbst auf dem Grund der Verzweiflung* (Frankfurt am Main: Suhrkamp, 1991); cf. also the Introduction and Theunissen's contribution to M. Theunissen and W. Greve, eds, *Materialien zur Philosophie Sören Kierkegaards* (Frankfurt am Main: Suhrkamp, 1979).

21 *Das Selbst auf dem Grund der Verzweiflung*, p. 25.

22 *Negative Theologie der Zeit*, p. 354. In this treatise on Jesus' conception of prayer Theunissen summarizes the reconstruction of Kierkegaard's argument which he has developed elsewhere: pp. 345ff.

23 Ibid., p. 359.

24 Ibid., p. 360.

25 I thank Lutz Wingert for his critical comments.

26 *Negative Theologie der Zeit*, p. 360.

27 To this context belong Theunissen's interesting studies of the way in which psychiatric patients experience time: 'Können wir in der Zeit glücklich sein?' and 'Melancholisches Leiden unter der Herrschaft der Zeit', in ibid., pp. 37–88 and 218–84. I read these attempts at a philosophical appropriation of the observations of psychologists (above all, in the school of Binswanger) as steps along the second of the three viable paths of philosophical thought which Theunissen has outlined.

28 *Negative Theologie der Zeit*, pp. 29–32.

29 J. Habermas, 'Was macht eine Lebensform "rational"?', in *Erläuterungen zur Diskursethik* (Frankfurt am Main, 1991), pp. 31–48.

30 'Society and History: A Critique of Critical Theory', p. 258.

31 M. Theunissen, *Selbstverwirklichung und Allgemeinheit* (Berlin: de Gruyter, 1982), p. 8.

32 'Society and History', p. 258; *Selbstverwirklichung und Allge-meinheit*, p. 27.
33 J. Habermas, 'Transzendenz von innen, Transzendenz ins Diesseits', in *Texte und Kontexte* (Frankfurt am Main: Suhrkamp, 1991), pp. 127–56.

8

The Useful Mole who Ruins the Beautiful Lawn

The Lessing Prize for Alexander Kluge

I

The Lessing Prize for Alexander Kluge – the constellation of these two names seems to make sense straightaway. But why something should make such obvious sense is, of course, not so easy to explain.

Clearly, Lessing and Kluge share a number of common traits. The dramatist developed his own dramaturgy, the script-writer and director is also his own film theorist. Both are committed to an aesthetics of reception. Lessing is convinced that the 'purpose of the fable...is the moral lesson'. Kluge describes learning processes which have a deadly outcome, but he is always guided by a notion of the right way of living, on which he stubbornly insists. And even Lessing's appeal to his readers at the end of the 95th section of the *Hamburg Dramaturgy* could have come from Kluge: 'My thoughts may seem less and less coherent, indeed they may even seem to contradict each other: but they are no more than thoughts in which they (the readers, the audience) may find material for their *own* thinking. My intention is only to sow *fermenta cognitionis*.' Seeds of knowledge – that is what these remarkable tales told in writing, sound and

---

Laudatio delivered on 25 September 1990.

image are intended to be. However much these stories reflect the horrors of the twentieth century, they still point towards the spirit of the eighteenth. Lessing, for example, considered Diderot to be the greatest authority since Aristotle, and Alexander Kluge's *Stalingrad Documentation* also ends with a sentence from Diderot. It runs: 'No one has a natural right to give orders to others.' And one thinks of Schincke, the head of sixth-form, who is always utterly at a loss when someone obeys him.

But despite the similarities, a gap of two hundred years has inevitably also left its mark. For example Kluge's friend and teacher Adorno had to come between him and Lessing, before he was able to start reflecing how much weakness it requires to be enlightened. What separates Kluge from Adorno, however, is the link to worldly pragmatism, a feeling for the achievement of small-scale successes, which is more typical of the old-style Enlightenment. Of course, Kluge is not naive: 'Someone is only vulnerable', he states, 'as long as he has a goal. For example, you never succeed with a woman when that is what you set out to do.' Yet Kluge never allows his sense of vulnerability to hold him back from a commitment to specific aims. Kluge devises projects, and is extremely good at it. The company name-plates which you walk past if you go to visit him at his office are authentic, not Kluge-esque fabrications, as one might suspect. Kluge the loner relies on the productive power of co-operation. It is not just the Oberhausen Manifesto, the passing of a law to encourage film production, the celebrated film 'Germany in Autumn', or the programme *Culture Tracks* on satellite TV, which testify to this. Rather, it is everything which lies concealed behind the mysterious logo 'dctp'. Kluge's co-operation with Oskar Negt, someone with a very different outlook, has resulted in products which have achieved the status of cult books for a whole generation of readers.

Such pragmatism poised on the brink of the abyss requires a certain trustfulness. Kluge is not easily discouraged – and he does not discourage others. Without making any concessions to the affirmative, he maintains a kind of fragile trust – and shares it with others. Of course, this is not the trust of those who confuse with reality whatever compensates for the untenability of the present state of affairs, whatever lends it an appearance of normality and coherence. It is also not the trust of others who pride themselves on their privileged access to the transcendent, and who proffer *amor fati* to a community of devotees. Neither does Kluge's trust rely on a critique which is confident of its prior insight into the path of history. Here again Kluge is at one with Lessing: *primus sapientiae gradus est, falsa intellegere.* Critique is the first – but of course *only* the first – step to wisdom: *secundus vera cognoscere.* Critique is not the whole of knowledge. What I am suggesting is that, since Kluge never had faith in the philosophy of history, such faith can never flip over in his work into a negativism which treats the whole as the untrue. Kluge mistrusts the whole in any shape or form. He breaks free from negative dialectics, without giving up its insights. And in this way he creates a breathing space for that precarious moment of trust which – despite everything – brings him close to Lessing.

II

There are good reasons to honour such an intellectual, particularly at a time when some intellectuals are accusing others of an unwillingness to come to terms with the state of the world, in all its loveliness. Of course, Wolf Biermann, Sarah Kirsch and company have every right to demand an explanation from those with whom they have shared a common history. But the eagerness of people in the West to draw up the balance sheet for intellectuals in the DDR is not matched, at least not in every case, by moral sensitivity towards a silence which is indeed difficult to distinguish from complicity. It seems to me that this eagerness still bears traces of the good old German hostility towards transcendent aspirations which come to grief on the rock of reality. It is not just silence of which the DDR intellectuals are accused. For the intellectuals in the West they function as stalking horses – as stand-ins for all those who have ever

committed themselves to a project which went beyond the
juste milieu, and promised an improvement in the state of
things. Stalinism is now assumed to have been traced back to
its real roots: those utopian impulses which hinder consensus. At last we will be rid of the planners of new futures,
of those who think they know better. A blast on the whistle
will banish the dream-weavers back into the private domain.
Poets will then write poetry again, thinkers will think,
scientists pursue their research, and statesmen run the
state – preferably to the sound of church bells. No one will
be allowed to meddle in anyone else's affairs. There will be
no pro and contra: the code which governs agreement and
disagreement will taken out of service.

But Kluge's code is not so easy to crack. He doesn't fit into
the pattern: no ambitious theory, no tell-tale posturing, no
polemics, no obvious signals or grand words. And yet he is
never without his rather old-fashioned collecting bowl,
searching for the trace elements of dispersed utopian energies. Kluge comes with a soft step, and simply waits for the
lacquer to peel off. It is the hairline cracks in the varnish
which betray the energies of repressed life. They only show
up in the plural, on the small scale of inconspicuous detail,
on the margins of everyday life, and in ways which are
entirely profane. Kluge's casuistical way of looking at the
administered world is not that of the detached entomologist;
it is the gaze of the irritated jurist, who observes the web and
the prey with a certain admiration for the deadly creativity of
the spider. But he observes them with the aim of finding an
escape route into the open for the twitching victim.

III

It was this searching gaze, always on the look-out for escape
routes, which explored the life stories of Anita G. and dis-
trict judge Korti. These were the stories which first made
Kluge's name when he was still a young civil servant. You
will recall the restless Anita G., a woman from a middle-class

background who now roams the city. Through her petty thieving, deception and fraud she brings down – as if deliberately – a wave of police persecution which breaks over her and her child, and eventually buries both of them. The author reconstructs this woman's attempts to escape, which somehow lead unerringly towards her nervous breakdown in a Rhineland prison hospital. He reconstructs these attempts at flight from the files of the state prosecutor, and he manages to make the delinquent's life history vibrate through the network of legal concepts. These concepts, which are designed for ascertaining facts and subsuming them under categories, penetrate everything. Private relations and experiences are processed in the categories of aiding-and-abetting and incitement, profit and intent. Yet the life impulses of this woman, her incomprehensible motives, anxieties and desires, form only a murky residue compared with the rigid clarity of this reconstruction. The state prosecutor wonders: 'Why can't this intelligent person order her affairs in a satisfactory manner? Why doesn't she find a man who can take care of her? Why doesn't she accept the facts as they stand? Doesn't she want to?' The world of the state prosecutor is not rational enough to permit an answer to such obvious questions. And this, the author suggests between the lines, is precisely the reason why these questions are posed. The solid ground of facts arches over to become a vessel enclosing life, a vessel in which life itself becomes no more than a residue.

The world of law is a world of bureaucracy. In one Kluge story after another bureaucracy stands convicted of its own irrational rationality. But this is not the end of the matter. The justice system is still guided by an idea. But because it has to barricade itself behind its bureaucratic defences in order to defend the notion of justice against the unjust world outside, it cannot help but pervert this idea. Just think of the criminal prosecutor – his name was Scheliha – who, in January 1945, amidst the chaos of the collapsing Eastern Front, set off on an official journey to the embattled town of Elbing. His task was to clear up a dubious murder case in accordance with the strict rules of the constitutional investigation process. In the course of a brief skirmish the relevant files go up in flames. And yet it is not the idea of justice itself which is distorted out of all recognition by this case of *'fiat justitia pereat mundus'*. Rather, it is a justice system with no sense of judgement, one which has lost contact with reality.

Kluge knows well how useful organizations can be, how they can be used to pull things off. And this means that he cannot help being impressed by the rational kernel of these artificial, legally organized systems of action. This sensitivity inhibits Kluge. For example, it makes him resistant to being swept *without reservations* towards to an exclusively kafkaesque verdict, when he looks back at the terrifying normality and adaptability of judge Korti. I quote:

> Around 1800 a newspaper article would have sufficed for Korti to be removed from office, while around 1900 a reform movement would have been needed. In 1962 [the date when the book was written] even an uprising might not have been enough to get rid of him. And who would start an uprising just for his sake? Thus Korti's end still stands a long way off: indeed, *at first sight*, Korti's end seems to get further and further away.

One must be careful not to assume some theological reservation lying concealed in this 'at first sight'. The reservation is born of a fragile trust, and is entirely profane.

IV

In other words, Kluge's way of considering things does not neglect how they appear from a great distance, or from close up. His gaze is focused on the contact points where the categories of law and organization intrude into people's lives. Patiently, he pulls apart the seams, and stumbles on the suppressed intelligence of everyday life, fantasies and sensitivities, sublime virtues and capacities. He discloses the everyday rationality of that subjugated knowledge, accumulated over generations, which is exploited by the grand systems. He finds a useful common sense even in the small print of the military service regulations. Kluge cites (or apparently cites, I should say): 'It is impossible to caution too emphatically against the use of alcohol as a means of protection against the cold. Alcohol expands the surface of the skin, and merely creates an illusion of warmth. It may only be distributed when there is an immediate prospect of a reasonably long stay in heated accommodation.'

Yet it is just this encompassing backdrop of a lifeworld which, taken on its own terms, is bristling with intelligence which makes the great events, the desolate state of history, so incomprehensible. This is what Gabi Teichert does not understand. She is the patriot, albeit one who never utters the word 'patriot', in what I regard as Kluge's finest film. She merely shrugs her shoulders when something which occurred at Stalingrad is presented as a necessary consequence of something else. Gabi Teichert, another of Kluge's female characters, is interested in the specific illogicality of history: 'After all,' she says, 'the men and their officers were obviously all in favour. When General Paulus *failed* to order a break-out, how could 3000 men have been stopped from retreating from the trap?' It couldn't have been a problem of communication, as far as she is concerned. To prove it, Gabi Teichert recalls a situation in April 1945, when word got around that a train loaded with coal and foodstuffs had arrived in Hamburg-Harburg: 'so that soon 9,000 women [women again] and youths with handcarts and sacks were hurrying to the spot. There was no way of proving how the message could have been passed around in so short a time.' That was in April 1945, of course – in between eras. The moment of catastrophe is also the moment of emancipation.

Kluge is interested in turning points, the moment when the fate of a battle, a war, an epoch is decided. Step by step he follows the way in which organizations prepared the disaster of Stalingrad – a massive military enterprise based not on intention and co-operation (that would be the good life), but on accident and the internal logic of systems. Of course, the enterprise was also dependent on unpredictable life-histories and their subjugated know-how. The military doctor at Stalingrad had everything under control; but he also had the the good luck to find an old miner amongst his orderlies, who constructed a seven-kilometre-long underground passage for him between the bunker containing the operating theatre and the bunker for patients recovering from surgery. The whole thing only works as long as the system has the lifeworld in its grip.

All this changes at the moment of catastrophe, when one organization, the *Wehrmacht*, collapses, and the next organization, the Russian prisoner-of-war camp, is not yet in place. This moment of total exhaustion, when one form of organization gives way to another, is the only instant of freedom. This is what connects the misery of February 1942 at the gates of Stalingrad with the aftermath of the traumatic air-raid on Halberstadt in April 1945. Kluge's imagination returns again and again to the zero hour, the fiction of freedom, the moment of anarchy when history holds its breath and the timetable for the *Reichsbahn* trains breaks down. Of course, he knows as well as Luhmann that the broken continuum will be restored, that the new forms of organization will be almost indistinguishable from what preceded them. But Kluge, undismayed, still pokes around for the fading sparks of freedom in the rubble of this platitude. Only functional systems have something like the property of ultra-stability. For Kluge this is like saying that only cockroaches will survive the next atom bomb.

V

For any observer with a perspective like Kluge's, the last twelve months of German history have supplied plentiful material. I imagine Kluge standing at the telescope and observing the troop movements since November or September 1989, just as he did in 1968 and 1977. Straining his eyes, he observes a happier counterpart to Stalingrad – 45 years after the end of hostilities, something like the end of the War. Once again, it is the peripeteia which interests him, the climax and reversal.

I imagine the scenario for a film project roughly as follows. It starts with the stubborn wishes and expectations, the practical reflections of those who gather in the churches, or slip away over the Hungarian border, but above all with the fears and hopes, the artful manoeuvres, of those who defy tanks in the open streets. Krenz appears as the grimace of a collapsing order. Then the fall of the Wall, the moment of liberation, the power of feelings. In the midst of the transition from one system of organization to another, exhaustion, relief, exuberance. Breaking into the Stasi buildings. Guarding the files. Attempts at reorientation, attempts to hold onto the state of transition for as long as possible. But the round table wobbles, it has no firm footing. One leg is too short, another has been sawn through with tools imported from the West. Now it is only good for spiritualist seances. Spectral work on a new constitution: swords into ploughshares – my God, is it so long ago already?

I imagine how Kluge, whose film, for good reasons, will be called 'German National Theatre', portrays the organization of happiness. The conquest by the West Goths. The taking over of the organizational network of the old minority parties, which had remained intact. The old comrades are the new comrades. Jubilant masses, decked out in black, gold and red. Ludwig Erhard and his dachshund. Proper majorities, proper timetables. The *Bundesbahn* administration sets up the rail connections. Schumpeter's process of creative destruction takes its course.

I imagine how Kluge, as always, finds a compressed symbol for the launch of the new form of organization. A Hamburg weekly starts a questionnaire on the theme of the new national day of celebration. A former supreme court judge would like to hold open the option of the day when a new constitution comes into force. Others would simply like to legalize the *de facto* day of celebration which the soccer triumph in Rome has provided. The majority of voters, however, are in favour of a national-bureacratic solution.

The smooth administrative achievement of unification is approved by the leading figures in the land: the state treaties whisked out of a little black box have forestalled any interference by the people and, for the most part, reduced parliament to silence. This neat, bureaucratically engineered unity must be crowned in an appropriate way. The cabinet gratefully takes up a suggestion from the intellectual world. It declares the name day of a minister who played a decisive role in the negotiations to be the holiday celebrating the rebirth of national unity.

I imagine that the book of the film will have lots of illustrations and contemporary documents. A boxed space is reserved for the pronouncement of one of our dear historians from the *Frankfurter Allgemeine Zeitung*: 'Only the nation can make the end of Communism bearable. The nation compensates for the evanescence of human things.' The next day, in *Le Monde*, Alain Touraine defends the category of society against the nationalist muddying of public consciousness. Kluge reserves another space for an interview with the civil rights lawyer Jens Reich in *Der Spiegel*. I quote: 'I am rather disappointed that the chandelier was cut down from the ceiling. The whole country has hit the ground with a crash. No one is going to persuade me that things had to happen like that.' Kluge and Reich attended the same school.

I imagine that Kluge revises his plans after a conversation with Jens Reich, sets off for Halberstadt to do some filming, and then hands over the material to his film-editor Beate Mainka-Jellinghaus for further work.

VI

Kluge is a master of the surreal tale, for in his view reality cannot be presented in any other way. One never knows whether what Kluge reports as fact is indeed fact. But the way he reports events makes clear that it really could have happened like that. I quote: 'Up until Spring 1942, the

reformers in the army had successfully argued that troop con-
tingents to the south of the Loire should be allowed to wear
the top button of their uniforms open in summer.' Anyone
who saw how Stefan Aust, very much in the spirit of Kluge,
presented the jars of human smells collected by the Stasi on
Spiegel TV, will no longer doubt Kluge's realism. In section 23
of the *Hamburg Dramaturgy* Lessing answers the question of
when the poet may depart from historical truth with the
words: 'In every case, for the poet only the characters are
holy.' Kluge shares Lessing's dramaturgical perspective on a
history which must be taken away from the historians.
Because, for the writer, only life stories are sacred, he has no
respect for the line between documentation and fiction. Only
if a story is scurrilous enough should we assume it is true.

VII

Kluge is also a master of montage, as you know, for the
interconnections of reality can only be shown through its
fragmentation. 'Eleven to eleven' is a title which recalls the
start of the carnival season. The programme usually begins
after eleven on Monday evenings, as if the programmers were
ashamed – eleven past eleven, rather than before eleven.
Every Monday evening, for a quarter of an hour on RTL,
Kluge stages the collapse of the elegant order which the TV
stations have spent the whole day setting up for their view-
ers. Lessing, as we know, gave the Aristotelian concept of
mimesis a new interpretation. Kluge revolutionizes the
notion of imitation once again: montage is a way of breaking
open the false continuum, and thereby reproducing the
effects of a catastrophe: 'In the instant of catastrophic disruption it becomes clear for a moment that the conditions of
existence are all awry – and that nowhere do they provide the
basis for human, or even viable, relations.' I have no doubt
that there can be few contemporary authors so deserving of
the prize which the city of Hamburg awards in the name of
Lessing.

Sources

The Liberating Power of Symbols
Die befreiende Kraft der symbolischen Formgebung. Lecture given on 20 April 1995 at the University of Hamburg, previously unpublished.

The Conflict of Beliefs
Vom Kampf der Glaubensmächte. Lecture given on 26 September 1995 at the University of Heidelberg, previously unpublished.

Between Traditions
Zwischen den Traditionen. A *laudatio* for Georg Henrik von Wright. Lecture given on 21 May 1996 at the University of Leipzig, previously unpublished.

Tracing the Other of History in History
In der Geschichte das Andere der Geschichte aufspüren, in *Babylon,* nos 10–11, 1992, pp. 139–45.

A Master Builder with Hermeneutic Tact
Ein Baumeister mit hermeneutischem Geschick. Frankfurter Rundschau, 16 May 1990.

Israel or Athens: Where does Anamnestic Reason Belong?
Israel oder Athen, in J. B. Metz et al., *Diagnosen der Zeit* (Düsseldorf: Patmos-Verlag, 1994), pp. 51–64.

Communicative Freedom and Negative Theology
Kommunikative Freiheit und negative Theologie, in E. Angehrn et al., *Dialektischer Negativismus* (Frankfurt am Main: Suhrkamp, 1992), pp. 15–34.

The Useful Mole who Ruins the Beautiful Lawn
Nützlicher Maulwurf. Frankfurter Rundschau, 29 September 1990.

Index

absolute, the 98; Cassirer and 27 n.; Theunissen, Hegel and 96

abstraction 19, 95

Adam 60

Adorno, Theodor W.: Kluge and 113; Theunissen and 92

Albert, Hans: Apel and 73

alienation 100

'Analytical Philosophy of Language and the Problem of the *Geisteswissenschaften*' (Apel) 71

anamnestic reason 80–4

'anticipatory' present 97

Apel, Karl-Otto 66–76

'Arcades Project' (Benjamin) 6, 58

Aristotle: 'phronesis' 53

art: freedom and abstraction 19; Warburg and creation 7

Aust, Stefan 122

authenticity (philosophy) 32, 38, 40, 43; self 90, 103, 107

autonomy 82

avant-garde, early modernist 6

bad continuity of history (Benjamin) 93

being-with-oneself-in-the-other (Hegel): Theunissen and 96–7, 98, 107

belief *see* faith and philosophy

Benjamin, Walter 93; Apel and 70; and recollection/reconciliation 81; Scholem and 58; Warburg and 6

biblical tradition 35–6

Binswanger, Ludwig: Theunissen and 110 n.

Buber, Martin: Theunissen and 91

capitalism 78, 100

Carnap, Rudolf: von Wright and 52

Cassirer, Ernst 1–26

Catholic Church 85–8; Metz and 78–9, 87–8

causality 47

ciphers: and faiths 36–7, 39

civilization, fundamental act of 7

Cohen, Hermann: Cassirer and 16

colonialism, European 85

communication: Apel and 72–4, 75–6; Jaspers and 31,43; Theunissen and 'communicative

communication (*contd*)
   freedom' 90, 94–102, 107;
   see also existentialism:
   communication
comparative religion: Jaspers
   and 36–44
conceptual systems 16
contextualism 33–4; Apel and
   76
critique: Kluge and 114;
   Marx's distinction between
   presentation and 96
The Critique of Judgement
   (Kant) 74
The Critique of Pure Reason
   (Kant) 4
cultures, clash of 30–1, 33–5,
   41–4

Davos disputation (Cassirer and
   Heidegger) 22–3
DDR 114–15, 120
democracy: Cassirer and 23;
   and the United Nations 30–1
deontology: Cassirer 24; von
   Wright 47, 51–2, 55
despair, existential 100–3, 106;
   confidence produced by
   turning against itself of
   93–4
Diderot, Denis: Lessing and 113
Dilthey, Wilhelm 5, 68
Diskurs und Verantwortung
   (Apel) 71
Dobrushka, Moses 64
domination 95; cultural,
   avoidance of 86, 87
Dostoyevsky, Fyodor 105

'Eleven to eleven' (German TV
   programme) 122
Enlightenment, the (Europe):
   and cultural pluralism 86–7;
   French Revolution 64; Kant
   and 74; Kluge and 113;
   Metz, religion and 79;

separation of faith and
   reason 35, 36–7, 42
ethics: discourse ethics 75;
   Jaspers and 38, 39, 43–4;
   philosophical essence 25;
   and physics 5–6; Theunissen
   and 105–6
existence and symbolization 17
existentialism 67–8;
   communication 31, 32, 39,
   41; confidence from
   despair 93–4; nature of
   philosophy 37–8; *see also*
   despair, existential; self, the
*Explanation and
   Understanding* (von
   Wright) 47

fable: Lessing on 112
faith and philosophy 35–8,
   39–42, 102, 104
faiths, struggle between 33, 36,
   39, 40–1, 42–4
Fichte, Johann Gotlieb:
   Theunissen, Kierkegaard
   and 91
Fortuna (symbol) 6
foundational role of
   philosophy 3–4
Frank, Jakob 63
*Frankfurter Allgemeine
   Zeitung* 121
freedom 102; Cassirer and 6,
   7–8; moral sense
   (Theunissen) 105; the
   Other (Theunissen) 97–8;
   self-realization 106–7;
   subjective 82; von Wright
   and 52–5; *see also*
   communication: Theunissen
   and 'communicative freedom'
Frege, Gottlob 12, 16, 18
French Revolution 64
Freud, Sigmund 6; and
   recollection 81; Scholem
   and 64

fundamentalism 43–4

Gadamer, Hans-Georg 31
German reunification: Kluge
  on 120–1
God: freedom 97–8, 102; Kant
  and 106; and the Other 102;
  Theunissen, Kierkegaard
  and 102, 104–5; *see also* faith
  and philosophy
The Great Philosophers
  (Jaspers) 32

Hagerström, Axel: Cassirer's
  study of 24
Hamburg Dramaturgy
  (Lessing) 112, 122
Hegel, G. W. F. 35; Cassirer
  and 4; Kierkegaard, Marx
  and 90; Theunissen and
  94–8, 102, 105–6
Heidegger, Martin 35; Apel
  and 67–8, 70, 71, 76; and
  Cassirer 22–3; Jaspers
  and 38; Theunissen and 94
Hellenization of
  Christianity 79–83, 92, 94
historicism 82, 84; Dilthey 5;
  distortions by 58, 64;
  German Historical
  School 63, 68;
  Marxism-Leninism 74–5;
  responses to 31, 33, 76, 95;
  Theunissen 92
Horkheimer, Max: Apel and 76
human rights: Cassirer and 23;
  cultural pluralism and
  (Metz) 86–7; and the United
  Nations 30–1
Humboldt, Wilhelm von 68;
  Cassirer and 12–14, 15–16,
  22

'The Idea of Language in the
  Tradition of Humanism'
  (Apel) 69

idealism 81, 82–3; anamnestic
  reason and 80, 83;
  Cassirer 22, 23
idealization: and validity-
  claims 99
*The Individual and the Cosmos
  in the Renaissance*
  (Cassirer) 6
intentionalist theories of
  meaning 53
intersubjectivity 82;
  Theunissen and 90–1, 94,
  95, 99, 102, 107–8
Introduction to Metaphysics
  (Apel) 68
Islam 31; Ṣevi's conversion 62

Jaspers, Karl 30–3; and the
  plurality of faiths 36–44
Jesus Christ: Theunissen
  and 110 n.
Judaism 26, 57–65; heritage in
  Christianity 79–83
'Judaism and the Modern
  Political Myths'
  (Cassirer) 26

Kabbalah 57–8, 59–60, 64–5;
  Nathan of Gaza 63
Kant, Immanuel: Apel and
  74; Cassirer and 4, 12,
  15–16, 23; Hegel and
  105–6; Humboldt and
  13; and reason 35;
  Theunissen and 104,
  105–6; von Wright and
  49, 53, 54, 55
'The Kantian Element in
  Wilhelm von Humboldt's
  Philosophy of Language'
  (Cassirer) 12
Kempski, J. von: Apel and, on
  Peirce 72
Kierkegaard, Søren: Jaspers
  and 37–8; Theunissen
  and 90, 91, 100–5

Kluge, Alexander 112–22

language, philosophy of:
Apel 69, 70, 71, 73–4;
Cassirer 9–20, 22, 24;
consciousness to
understanding 99; Hegel
and 96; Heidegger 71;
Humboldt 12–14, 15–16,
68; Jaspers and 44;
Theunissen and 96, 110 *n.*;
transcendence 98;
Wittgenstein 71
'Language and Myth'
(Cassirer) 9–12
law, theory of 23–4
Lessing, Gotthold Ephraim:
Apel and 71; Kluge
and 112–14, 122
liberation 82;
communicative 98; *see also*
freedom
Litt, Theodor: Apel and 68
logic: Cassirer and 5;
Theunissen and Hegel's
Logic 94–8
logos mysticism 69–70
'loss, culture of' (Metz) 83
Luria, Isaak 59–61
Luther, Martin: Zwingli and
37

MacIntyre, Alasdair 34
*The Main Currents of
Jewish Mysticism*
(Scholem) 57
Marc-Wogau, Konrad: Cassirer
and 20
Marx, Karl: Apel and 71;
Scholem and 64; Theunissen
and 90, 91, 96, 100; von
Wright and 49
Marxism-Leninism 74–5
Meggle, Georg 52, 53
Messiah, the 61–3
metaphor 11, 18

Metz, Johann Baptist 78–88;
Theunissen and 92
mimesis/imitation: Kluge,
Lessing and 122
'Mnemosyne' (keyword:
Warburg) 6–7
Moltmann, Jürgen: Theunissen
and 92
monotheistic religions 19; *see
also individual religions*
montage: Kluge 122
moral duty: Theunissen
and 105–6; von Wright
and 54–5
Musil, Robert: von Wright
and 49
myth: images 9, 10–12, 19, 24;
philosophers and 32, 36; and
symbolic forms 20;
totalitarianism and 25–6

Nathan of Gaza 61–3, 65
Nazis 25–6
'negative dialectics' (Adorno)
92; Kluge and 114
negative theology 36;
Theunissen 95–109
Negt, Oskar 113
neo-positivism: Apel and 71
Nicholas of Cusa: Cassirer
and 5
Nietzsche, Friedrich: and
Hellenized Christianity 83
1989 (Germany) 119–20
norms: Metz and 84;
Theunissen and 98–100; von
Wright and 51–6

objectification (linguistics)
15–16, 18–19, 24
objectivity, absolute:
Theunissen 107–8
Other, the: radically/sheerly
Other (Theunissen)
97–8, 102; and the self 96–7,
101

'ought', the: inversion 99–100; Theunissen and 99–100, 105–6

pagan antiquity: Warburg and 6–7
Peirce, Charles Sanders: Apel and 70, 71–2
Philosophical Investigations (Wittgenstein) 50
'phronesis' (Aristotle) 53
Philosophy of Symbolic Forms (Cassirer) 2, 7
physics: Cassirer and 5–6
Platonism: Jaspers and 32
pluralism, cultural: the Catholic Church and 85–8
Popper, Karl: Apel and 76
postmodernism: Apel and 76
The Problem of Knowledge in the Philosophy and Science of the Modern Age (Cassirer) 5
'The Problem of Ultimate Philosophical Justification in the Light of a Transcendental Pragmatics of Language' (Apel) 73
prolepsis 89 n., 94

Rawls, John: and Jaspers 40–1
reception, aesthetics of 112
recognition: culture of (Metz) 87–8; reciprocal (Theunissen) 95–6
recollection 81; *see also* anamnestic reason
reconciliation: communicative freedom and 100; God as structure of 97
Reconquista (Spain) 60
reflection, model of: Theunissen, Hegel and 96
Reich, Jens 121
relativism 33
Renaissance, the: Warburg and 6–7

revelation: Jaspers and 37
Rorty, Richard 34; Apel and 69, 76
Rothacker, Erich 67, 68, 70
Russell, Bertrand 16

Sabbatai Ṣevi (Scholem) 57–65
salvation 79, 81, 109; and cultural pluralism 86–7; Jewish exile and 60–1; Theunissen and 92–5
Sartre, Jean-Paul 67
Scheler, Max: Apel and 70
Schelling, F. W. J. von: Jaspers and 32
Scholem, Gershom 26, 57–65
Schumpeter, Joseph A. 120
'scientific method' 35
'Scientism or Transcendental Hermeneutics?' (Apel) 72–3
self, the 38, 39; abandonment and freedom 98; authenticity 90; distancing from external world 7; Kierkegaard and 100–4; realization 106; Theunissen and 100–4, 106–7
self-determining life, anthropology of the 49
sense impressions 21
Ṣevi, Sabbatai 59, 62–3
The Sickness unto Death (Kierkegaard): Theunissen and 98–102
signs and semiotics 21; Apel 72; Cassirer and Kant 12, 16; *see also* ciphers
socialized subjects 82
speech acts 53
Spengler, Oswald: Wittgenstein and 49–50
Stalingrad Documentation (Kluge) 113, 118–19
Stalinism 115

story-telling 83; Kluge
112–13, 115–17, 118–22
symbols and symbolization 3,
7–26

technology: totalitarianism
and 25
theodicy 59, 83–5, 96
theoretical sciences: linguistic
independence 18
Theunissen, Michael 90–109
'thing-in-itself' 16–17, 20–1
time: Theunissen and 93–4,
109 *n.*
totalitarianism 25–6
Touraine, Alain 121
Tractatus Logico-Philosophicus
(Wittgenstein) 12, 50
transcendence: God and
language 98; (Jaspers)
38–9; Theunissen,
Kierkegaard and
103–5
transcendental subject,
the: Apel and 72; Humboldt
and 13–14;symbolization 21
Transformation of Philosophy
(Apel) 71
trust: Kluge 113–14, 117
tsim-tsum (Luria) 60

'unanimity' (Jaspers) 32, 43

United Nations, the 30–1
universalism 33; Metz and 86,
88
Usener, Hermann: Cassirer
and 9, 10
utopia 75, 115

'Vermischte Bemerkungen'
(Wittgenstein) 49
Vienna Circle: and
Wittgenstein 50

Warburg, Aby 1–3, 6–7;
Cassirer and 6–7, 11, 24
Warburg Library 1–6, 9
Weber, Max 30, 53
Weimar Republic: Cassirer
and 17, 23
whole, the: Kluge and 114
Wittgenstein, Ludwig 12;
Apel and 71, 76; von Wright
and 48, 49–50, 53
World War II: Kluge and
116–17, 118–19, 121–2; and
subsequent philosophical
climate 67
Wright, Georg Henrik von
46–56

Zohar, the: Luria and 59
Zwingli, Huldrich: Jaspers
and 37